THE SHOOTING SCRIPT
MARGOT AT THE WEDDING

MARGOT AT THE WEDDING

SCREENPLAY BY NOAH BAUMBACH

INTRODUCTION BY PATRICIA BOSWORTH

A Newmarket Shooting Script® Series Book
NEWMARKET PRESS • NEW YORK

Screenplay, Motion Picture Artwork, and Photography ™ & © 2007 by Paramount Vantage. All rights reserved.

Introduction copyright © 2007 by Patricia Bosworth

Q & A with Noah Baumbach copyright © 2007 by Rob Feld

All rights reserved. Used by permission.

The Newmarket Shooting Script® Series is a registered trademark of Newmarket Publishing & Communications Company.

This book is published simultaneously in the United States of America and in Canada.

All rights reserved. This book may not be reproduced, in whole or in part, in any form, without written permission. Inquiries should be addressed to: Permissions Department, Newmarket Press, 18 East 48th Street, New York, NY 10017.

FIRST EDITION

10 9 8 7 6 5 4 3 2 1

ISBN: 978-1-55704-793-9

Library of Congress Catalog-in-Publication Data available upon request.

QUANTITY PURCHASES

Companies, professional groups, clubs, and other organizations may qualify for special terms when ordering quantities of this title. For information, write to Special Sales, Newmarket Press, 18 East 48th Street, New York, NY 10017; call (212) 832-3575 or 1-800-669-3903; FAX (212) 832-3629; or e-mail info@newmarketpress.com.

Website: www.newmarketpress.com

Manufactured in the United States of America.

OTHER BOOKS IN THE NEWMARKET SHOOTING SCRIPT® SERIES INCLUDE:

About a Boy: The Shooting Script	In Good Company: The Shooting Script
Adaptation: The Shooting Script	Little Miss Sunshine: The Shooting Script
The Age of Innocence: The Shooting Script	Man on the Moon: The Shooting Script
American Beauty: The Shooting Script	The Matrix: The Shooting Script
A Beautiful Mind: The Shooting Script	Michael Clayton: The Shooting Script
Big Fish: The Shooting Script	The People vs. Larry Flynt: The Shooting Script
The Birdcage: The Shooting Script	Pieces of April: The Shooting Script
Black Hawk Down: The Shooting Script	Punch-Drunk Love: The Shooting Script
Capote: The Shooting Script	Red Dragon: The Shooting Script
Cast Away: The Shooting Script	The Shawshank Redemption: The Shooting Script
Cinderella Man: The Shooting Script	Sideways: The Shooting Script
The Constant Gardener: The Shooting Script	Snow Falling on Cedars: The Shooting Script
Dead Man Walking: The Shooting Script	The Squid and the Whale: The Shooting Script
Eternal Sunshine of the Spotless Mind: The Shooting Script	State and Main: The Shooting Script
	Stranger Than Fiction: The Shooting Script
Gods and Monsters: The Shooting Script	Traffic: The Shooting Script
Gosford Park: The Shooting Script	Transamerica: The Shooting Script
Human Nature: The Shooting Script	The Truman Show: The Shooting Script
The Ice Storm: The Shooting Script	War of the Worlds: The Shooting Script

OTHER NEWMARKET PICTORIAL MOVIEBOOKS AND NEWMARKET INSIDER FILM BOOKS INCLUDE:

The Art of The Matrix*	A Good Year: Portrait of the Film
The Art of X2*	Hitchhiker's Guide to the Galaxy: The Filming of the Douglas Adams Classic
The Art of X-Men: The Last Stand	
Bram Stoker's Dracula: The Film and the Legend*	Hotel Rwanda: Bringing the True Story of an African Hero to Film*
Chicago: The Movie and Lyrics*	The Jaws Log
Dances with Wolves: The Illustrated Story of the Epic Film*	Kinsey: Public and Private*
Dreamgirls	Memoirs of a Geisha: A Portrait of the Film
E.T. The Extra-Terrestrial: From Concept to Classic*	Ray: A Tribute to the Movie, the Music, and the Man*
Gladiator: The Making of the Ridley Scott Epic Film	Saving Private Ryan: The Men, The Mission, The Movie
Good Night, and Good Luck: The Screenplay and History Behind the Landmark Movie*	Schindler's List: Images of the Steven Spielberg Film
	Tim Burton's Corpse Bride: An Invitation to the Wedding

*Includes Screenplay

CONTENTS

Introduction by Patricia Bosworth	vii
The Shooting Script	1
Stills	following page 84
Q & A with Noah Baumbach	109
Cast and Crew Credits	123
About the Writer/Director	129

Introduction

by Patricia Bosworth

Camera always moving, reframing the action, soundtrack crowded with voices and natural sounds. Opening images: young boy screaming his head off between the cars of a hurtling train. Poisoned relationships. Family secrets. Broken promises. Three sisters (one fat and never seen). Scenes moving so fast they seem to crash into each other. Everybody haunted. Autumn leaves crunching underfoot. A pig is slaughtered. Rude, dirty, mean neighbors. A dog named Wizard keeps getting lost. Soft music playing. You have to pay attention to all the characters, adults and children, because they are all equally interesting. In despair but resourceful. Somehow they embrace life ... they take a step forward and take a step back. What was it a character from Chekhov said? When reminded of a crisis he is told, "Everything passes," and he replies, "Nothing passes."

These are just a few jottings I scrawl in a notebook as I watch *Margot at the Wedding*, Noah Baumbach's singular vision of family dysfunction.

I'm afraid to say how good this movie is because then people may expect too much or want something different, and it won't be to everybody's taste; this movie doesn't sentimentalize. The characters aren't self-pitying. But Baumbach just assumes the intelligence of the audience, assumes we don't need to have basic emotions spelled out for us. As a result, though, when you see *Margot at the Wedding,* you might recognize aspects of yourself.

The movie begins as Margot arrives for her sister Pauline's wedding, to be held within the next few days in the family's ramshackle country house overlooking a long blue bay. The two sisters haven't spoken in several years,

---

Patricia Bosworth is a contributing editor of *Vanity Fair* and the author of biographies of Montgomery Clift, Diane Arbus, and Marlon Brando.

so tension is high. In fact, when the two first embrace, there's a kind of manic pain in the air; the embrace is fierce and quick and gingerly. It's as if the women are literally too hot to handle.

This is essentially the story of two sisters, but it touches on their rivalry and competitiveness and their closeness indirectly.

There are several universal themes we can relate to here ... love destroyed by competition, sisters in opposition ... so deep and pervasive, the broad outlines polarize with a passion and ambivalence. But nothing is ever resolved. Will Margot really leave her marriage and be an independent woman? Will Pauline marry Malcolm or give him up or have the baby and stay in the house? This is a movie about women's choices and the endless possibilities we all have and the tragedies that ensue when we ignore them.

Nicole Kidman as Margot brings to the character a full measure of dread and awareness. She plays an edgy, high-strung writer, an incipient alcoholic (she's never without that goblet of iced wine). She looks terrific, reed-slim, immaculate, usually bespectacled, given to masturbating unsuccessfully in the dark ... and throughout the movie she tries to control every situation until she drives her whole family up the wall. Whereas her sister Pauline ("Paul," eloquently played by Jennifer Jason Leigh) is a warm, messy, sensual former hippie, in awe of but angry at her sister's interference and imperiousness. Paul wears oversize men's striped pajamas with the jacket open to reveal a glimpse of her shapely breasts.

The scenes between the sisters appear improvised, unplanned, the dialogue often so brief and elliptical that the women seem to be speaking in a private language all their own. Then you read the screenplay and it is so beautifully written and carefully thought-out that you realize nothing has been left to chance.

The same is true in the scenes with the children; they seem improvised. Every kid is such a presence in the movie. The interplay between them and the adults is terrific. The children's world of fragmented understanding and misunderstanding overlaps the grown-ups' world of understanding and misunderstanding through lies, deceptions, evasions.

Zane Pais (Margot's son) is especially endearing. He is in turn confused, melancholy, depressed, skeptical, and hurting, especially when his mother gives him cruel, mixed messages. Zane keeps the atmosphere very raw by his responses. He's part of why the movie really gets you. You see everything from his point of view.

And all the other characters are vivid, alive, eccentric, unexpected, too (even the angry, cursing mother in the woods Margot tries to give advice to). As for Jack Black as Malcolm, he is remarkable as Pauline's schlub of a husband-to-be. He lets his insecurities hang out, but manages to be endearing and sexy. He's the sanest person in this crazy family! And all the while you see his emotions just fermenting inside of him, emotions he isn't conscious of until they explode.

Before I finish this introduction I meet Noah Baumbach at his favorite café in Greenwich Village, Bar Pitti. It's a hot, humid afternoon the day before the opening of the New York Film Festival.

We sit eating panini and drinking caffe latte, and then we talk process and craft, how he wrote *Margot* (in many drafts), "and yes, Jennifer [his wife] read every draft."

I tell Noah my favorite scene is the library scene where Margot is being interviewed about her writing in front of an audience, and she's talking about her father, who was both abusive and loving (you really get the picture of why this woman is so damaged), and suddenly the interviewer, who may be her new lover, asks her, Could the father, in fact, be a portrait of you? And she just loses it and starts sweating and babbling crazily, and then is appalled at what the question has aroused in her and she staggers off to the ladies room to cry hysterically.

I ask Noah what character he feels closest to, and he answers, "Margot, c'est moi!" And in the next breath, "I'm kidding." He's been accused of cannibalizing his family in *The Squid and the Whale* so much, he admits he wrote that particular scene in response.

I'm reminded of what John Guare said once: "When you write you get to play all the parts." So Noah is probably a combination of many of his characters in his writing.

After we say goodbye, I walk through the bustling, teeming Village streets thinking of all the inexhaustible possibilities in film. The story of Margot and her family *seems* simple, but Noah has posed universal questions in a different way. There's an elusiveness and unpredictability about *Margot at the Wedding*. It makes me eager to find out what he's going to come up with next.

Margot at the Wedding

by

Noah Baumbach

April 10, 2006

1   INT. TRAIN CAR - DAY   1

A cashier hands a boy, 13, his change across a counter. The boy stuffs the coins in his pocket. He lifts the cardboard tray with two hot dogs, a bag of chips, and two Cokes. This is Claude.

We follow him: He carefully carries the meal down the aisle, balances it in one hand as he opens the door.

The train noise blares as he traverses the area between cars.

He enters the new car repeating the balancing act. He waits while a man shoves his back-pack onto the metal rack above the seats. Claude hurries a bit more now, his concentration alternating between the food and the path.

He sits next to a brunette woman. He hands her a hot dog.

                    CLAUDE
          Here.

He's met by a severe and pinched face. The eyes have black circles -- there is a scar above her lip. Claude instantly blushes and mumbles:

                    CLAUDE
          Sorry.

He gets up and hurries a few seats further. He slides next to a pretty brunette woman, late 30's, with straight shoulder length hair. Her name is Margot.

                    MARGOT
          That was quick.

                    CLAUDE
          I sat next to the wrong person.

                    MARGOT
          Really? Where?

She stretches up and peers over the seats. He grabs her shirt.

                    CLAUDE
          Please don't look. She'll see you.

                    MARGOT
          Careful with my blouse.

2   CUT TO: 2

Margot is sleeping, her head against the window. Claude listens to his iPod. He takes out the earphones, gets up, and walks to the front of the car. Opens the door and goes between cars.

The train roars and screeches. Claude screams. He stops, looks around. He screams again.

3   CUT TO: 3

Claude and his mother gaze out the dirt streaked window at a river. An old castle-like structure emerges from the water.

Houses are run-down. In the distance there's a power plant. Electrical lines crisscross the sky. Claude puts his finger against the glass and traces the wires.

      CLAUDE
Will the wedding be crowded?

      MARGOT
I don't know. I think she doesn't know anyone anymore.

      CLAUDE
How long has she known Malcolm?

      MARGOT
Only a year.

      CLAUDE
Is that short?

      MARGOT
  (pointedly)
Would you marry someone you'd only known a year?

      CLAUDE
I'm not going to ever get married.

      MARGOT
I can't say I have a lot of hope for the whole thing.

      CLAUDE
Why are we going then?

      MARGOT
We're supporting her.

CLAUDE
I thought she wasn't speaking to you.

MARGOT
No...no...I wasn't speaking to her, but I'm over it.

4   EXT. FERRY DOCK - DAY   4

A ferry is docked. Cars pull up onto the boat. Margot runs, clutching a suitcase, holding down a floppy wine colored sun hat. Claude hurries alongside her, a bag slung over his shoulder.

5   EXT. FERRY - DAY   5

The rumbling and sputtering of the boat. People get out of their cars and stretch their legs.

Claude leans against the rail and lets the spray hit his face. Margot's cell vibrates. The caller ID: HOME. She stuffs the phone in her pocket.

MARGOT
Why aren't you wearing your new shades?

CLAUDE
I don't think I need them right now.

MARGOT
You begged for those glasses.

CLAUDE
I know, but...I will wear them, I just feel like people might think it's weird that a kid is wearing dark shades.

MARGOT
That's ridiculous.

Claude reluctantly takes out a pair of thin wrap-around punk sunglasses and puts them on. He looks around self-consciously.

MARGOT
You look very cool.

He takes them off.

                    CLAUDE
          I don't need them right now.

6   CUT TO: 6

     Margot and Claude wait. The ferry has emptied out.

                    CLAUDE
          Do they know we're here?

     A maroon Volvo station wagon peels around a bend and stops
     across the road. Two eyes peer out from just below the
     backseat window. A man, 40, in dumpy cargo shorts rolls down
     the window. He has a small moustache -- he's harried and
     sweaty. This is Malcolm. He points at Margot and Claude.

                    MALCOLM
          Are you...?

7   INT. VOLVO - DAY   7

     Malcolm drives. He smokes with the window open. Margot is
     in the passenger seat. In the back, Claude and the girl,
     Ingrid, sit shyly, their hair blows turbulently in the wind.
     Ingrid, 11, wears shorts, sandals, and a batik shirt with a
     panda on it.

                    MALCOLM
          Paul apologizes for not coming,
          she's still getting the house
          ready.

                    MARGOT
          I'm sorry it was such short notice.

                    MALCOLM
          I don't care. Paul's frantic, but
          I don't give a shit. Oh, and
          Ingrid wants me to tell you that
          she made us all bracelets.

                    INGRID
               (embarrassed)
          No, I wanted...I wanted to wait...

                    MALCOLM
          Oh, I thought you asked me to tell
          them. Anyway...

     Malcolm holds up his wrist and shows a knit blue and orange
     bracelet.

MALCOLM
I got Knicks colors.

INGRID
They're not Knicks colors!

MARGOT
It's beautiful, Ingrid.

INGRID
(to Claude)
I made this one for myself.

She shows him the purple and green one around her wrist.

INGRID
Yours is yellow. Is that okay?

CLAUDE
I guess.

INGRID
Where's your dad and Josh?

CLAUDE
They might come later.

MARGOT
Josh's spring break is next week.
Jim teaches through Friday and then
they open the house in Vermont on
the weekend.

MALCOLM
(bluntly)
It means a lot to Pauline that
you're here.

Margot nods awkwardly -- she blushes.

MARGOT
Oh. Good.

A car suddenly pulls out of a driveway, but nowhere near
their car. Malcolm swerves anyway.

MALCOLM
Holy Jesus! Watch it, dicksack!

Ingrid giggles. Margot clutches the handle above the door.

MALCOLM
If you're wondering about the
moustache --

MARGOT
No, I wasn't.

MALCOLM
I had a full beard for a while and
then when I shaved it I left this
part for last, you know to see how
it looked, and... It's meant to be
funny.

Margot nods politely. The sound of tires on gravel:

8   EXT. HOUSE - DAY   8

The trunk slams shut. The Volvo is parked in a driveway
alongside a grey Colonial house that sits above the water.
They lift bags. An old mutt ambles toward them.

Pauline emerges from the house. She's pretty like her
sister, late 30's. She walks briskly toward them. Margot
smiles and opens her arms, but Pauline passes her and dips
down to embrace Claude. She kisses him on the lips.

PAULINE
You're so handsome.

Now she hugs Margot. They both tear up. Claude beams.

PAULINE
I never thought I'd get you here.

A loud thud. They all turn toward the property fence. A
large pile of dead flowers and rotting plants has been dumped
into their yard. There's whispering and movement through
brush on the other side. Margot looks at Pauline with
concern.

PAULINE
You're arriving in the midst of a
drama. Ingrid, make sure Wizard is
inside.

Malcolm trudges over to the trash cans.

INGRID
It's the Voglers.

                    PAULINE
          The neighbors want us to cut down
          our tree.

She indicates a large oak that extends up and into the
adjoining property.

                    MARGOT
          No, that's our tree!

                    INGRID
          They think it's sick and rotting
          their property.

                    PAULINE
          We're having the ceremony under it.

                    MARGOT
          You took the swing down.

                    MALCOLM
          Pauline thinks this is their way of
          trying to be friends. I think they
          resent us because we're...

He searches for the word, but can't come up with anything.
He says wearily:

                    MALCOLM
          I don't know what we are.

9   INT. CLAUDE'S GUEST ROOM/INGRID'S ROOM - DAY   9

Claude sits on the squeaky bed, a yellow bracelet on his
wrist. An old flip-clock hums on the night-table. A door
opens onto a bathroom which has another door open onto
another bedroom.

Ingrid sits on her bed observing Claude. She holds a
realistic-looking stuffed rooster in an old-style tuxedo.

                    INGRID
          This is my room.

                    CLAUDE
          Okay.

                    INGRID
          Do you like showers or baths?

                    CLAUDE
          Showers. What about you?

Ingrid shrugs. She says, already bored with the topic:

                    INGRID
I don't care.

10   INT. STAIRWELL/MARGOT'S GUEST ROOM - DAY   10

Pauline and Margot carry bags up the stairs. Margot now wears a knit red bracelet. They're tentative with one another.

                    PAULINE
Is Malcolm what you thought he'd be?

                    MARGOT
Well, I didn't know what to --

                    PAULINE
The moustache is temporary. He left it for last when he was shaving. It's meant to be funny.

                    MARGOT
He told me.

                    PAULINE
Yeah...

They enter the guest room. The windows are wide open, the curtains blowing, but the room is very neatly made up.

                    PAULINE
I'm sorry -- with so little time to prepare, we had to put you in Malcolm's storage room --

                    MARGOT
This was Becky's room. Poor Becky.

                    PAULINE
Yeah, poor Becky. Now it's a storage room. I've just started to feel like it's our house not my parents. You know?

                    MARGOT
Our parents.

                    PAULINE
Of course. It might still smell like paint, but...

MARGOT
I thought he was a musician.

Pauline jimmies down the stiff windows. Margot begins to unpack and hang up clothes in the closet.

PAULINE
Well, music's officially a hobby... He's painting now. And writing letters to newspapers and magazines. He's very meticulous, he'll spend up to a week writing a response to a music review. He's incredibly smart. Maybe too smart. I don't know. We're doing very well.

MARGOT
Good. I mean, you must be.

Silence.

PAULINE
I don't know where to begin. What can I tell you? It seems I'm pregnant, but it's really early so... I haven't told anyone. I mean, I haven't told Malcolm or Ingrid.

MARGOT
Wow...

PAULINE
Yeah, if it sticks. We'll see. I hope so. Things are good. We did a couples seminar two months ago or so in Maine. They give you exercises and things to do. I know you're not convinced, but...

MARGOT
(vaguely)
Mm hm.

PAULINE
We got engaged right afterwards. The guy who runs it, Strickland, wrote a really interesting book about loving which I'll lend you if you want.

MARGOT
(non-committal)
Okay.

PAULINE
But only if you'll read it. Because I need it back. I made notes in the margins.

MARGOT
I may not get to it for a while.

PAULINE
Well, I'm not going to lend it to you if you're not going to read it.

They meet eyes. Pauline quickly turns away.

PAULINE
It's going to be very informal by the way. Just Mom and Becky. Malcolm's brother. Few friends. And now you and Claude. Nothing like the first one.

MARGOT
(wary)
Becky's coming?

PAULINE/MARGOT
She isn't how you.../I'd really like...

PAULINE
You go.

MARGOT
I was going to say, "I'd really like some white wine."

PAULINE
Oh. Yeah. We have a... Well...I'm glad you changed your mind and came. I never heard from you after I sent the invite...I even wondered if you got it.

MARGOT
(quickly)
Well, I'm so pleased we're here.

PAULINE
Did you get it?

                    MARGOT
          Yeah.

Pauline waits for an explanation.

                    MARGOT
          I'm sorry you were so angry...

                    PAULINE
          I wasn't angry. I
          was...disappointed.

                    MARGOT
          Uh huh. But you see when you say,
          "disappointed" it puts me in a
          crummy situation. Like I let you
          down.

                    PAULINE
          But you did in a way.

                    MARGOT
          I don't see it like that.

                    PAULINE
          Fine. I felt betrayed. Is that
          word okay?

                    MARGOT
          Again, you're making me the
          aggressor.

                    PAULINE
          You _were_ the aggressor.
               (pause)
          Let's not... I've become a really
          good cook.

11   INT. LIVING ROOM - LATE DAY   11

     Malcolm strums his guitar and smokes. Pauline sits at his
     feet with Ingrid and Claude. The kids look at a record
     sleeve. Margot is curled up on the sofa writing in a little
     brown notebook. She wears oval tortoise-shell glasses.

                    MARGOT
          I can't believe you've still got
          all of our old records.

     Ingrid pulls an album toward her. Her eyes widen at the
     scary image on the cover. She quickly turns it over and
     hands it to her mother.

INGRID
Mom, can you hide this please.

Pauline puts the record sleeve on top of a shelf.

PAULINE
(for Margot's benefit)
Malcolm played with Ric Ocasek once?

MALCOLM
In the late '80's. It was a solo gig after he left the Cars.

CLAUDE
So, you're kind of famous.

Malcolm reddens.

MALCOLM
No. No. Believe me, I'm not. I used to want to be, but, No. Do you want to be famous?

MARGOT
Claude wants to be very famous.

MALCOLM
Well, make sure you can handle rejection. I can't. For me, expectation just turns to disappointment. So, ultimately I'd rather not try. It'll all go black for us soon enough anyway.

PAULINE
Claude, ignore him.

Pauline sneaks a look at Margot who is watching Malcolm with an expression of either contempt or confusion. Pauline grows uncomfortable. She says to Claude:

PAULINE
When your mother moved to New York she used to send me books and records. She sent me REM's Murmur...

MARGOT
And the Pixies.

PAULINE
And X. She was very cool your
mother.

MARGOT
You only liked top forty.

PAULINE
Yeah, but I love REM now.

Margot takes off her reading glasses and rubs her eyes.

MARGOT
I don't really listen to music
anymore.

PAULINE
I was dating that guy, Horace back
then. Remember him?

MARGOT
Was that the guy who liked to rough
you up?

PAULINE
No, that was our dad.

Pauline and Margot crack up laughing. Malcolm raises an eyebrow at Claude.

MARGOT
Our father used to strip down to
his skivvies and beat us with a
belt.

MALCOLM
That man had a sexual screw loose.

PAULINE
It's awful -- that stuff that
happens to kids. Malcolm was
fondled by a male baby-sitter.

MALCOLM
Just use that information however
you want...

PAULINE
Sorry. We're with family. I
figured...

Claude looks at Malcolm. Malcolm doesn't meet his eyes.

                    PAULINE
          I think Becky got it the worst.

                    MARGOT
          Did she ever. Raped by the horse
          trainer...

Margot breaks into laughter. Pauline spits her seltzer back into the glass. They both laugh hysterically. Tears stream down Margot's face. Claude watches.

12   EXT. PATIO - NIGHT   12

     Malcolm, Pauline, Margot, Claude and Ingrid sit with a homosexual couple, Alan, 40's, and Toby, 30's, and their son, Bruce, 8, at an old wooden table eating crab, salad and soup. Part of Alan's face is paralyzed.

                    TOBY
          Alan rolled over in bed and looked
          at me and he said I can't feel my
          face. It took three doctors before
          we knew it was Bells Palsy.

                    ALAN
          They say a brush of wind can do it.

                    TOBY
          Feeling is slowly coming back.

                    MALCOLM
          We're all getting older... Which
          is terrible -- I don't care how
          universal it is. I can't remember
          names anymore.

                    MARGOT
          I have that. I blank out on
          certain words now too. Like the
          other day, I couldn't remember the
          word for...
              (laughs)
          I've forgotten it again. The stuff
          in wine. Sediment! That was it.

                    MALCOLM
          I know that. I was talking more
          about not remembering who was the
          bassist for Motley Crüe.

Malcolm lights up a cigarette. He offers one to Claude who shakes his head, No.

PAULINE
Ingrid, why don't you show Claude
and Bruce the game trunk.

INGRID
Okay.

Claude reluctantly follows Ingrid and Bruce. He looks back longingly at the table of adults.

MALCOLM
(relieved, to himself)
Mick Mars.

MARGOT
Toby, I think you need to have
Bruce diagnosed.

TOBY
Margot, I don't want to have this
conversation with you.

We follow the kids inside. We hear in the background:

MARGOT
It's vital. If you keep telling
him he's like everyone else he'll
wonder why he isn't. He's
suffering.

TOBY
He's tested very well. He does B's
in school.

Claude stops -- his mother and Toby are arguing out the window. Her eyes meet his for a second -- they make no connection -- she goes back to Toby.

MARGOT
But, that's how autism works. One
part of the brain can work fine
while the other is damaged.

ALAN
We had him diagnosed, Margot.
Nothing was found wrong.

MARGOT
Did you really, though?

TOBY
I'm...I'm not going to have this
conversation. I'm sorry.

Silence.

>   MARGOT
> I know it must be so difficult for
> you, but I think you have to --

13   INT. KITCHEN - SAME   13

Pauline unloads the plates onto the kitchen counter. She hesitates and exhales a deep, anxious breath.

14   EXT. HOUSE - NIGHT   14

Margot paces while talking on a cell phone in the herb garden. She drinks a white wine with ice cubes and smokes a joint. The bottle lies at her feet, three-quarters empty.

>   JIM'S VOICE
> What are you doing?

>   MARGOT
> I left you a note.

>   JIM'S VOICE
> Come back. Or meet me in Vermont
> on Saturday.

>   MARGOT
> No...no. The wedding is on
> Saturday. I'm here for that. I
> can't really pull out. How would
> that look?

>   JIM'S VOICE
> You haven't spoken to her in years --

>   MARGOT
> Well, we're speaking now. She is
> my closest friend despite it all...
> You're the one who's been trying to
> get me to call her.

>   JIM'S VOICE
> Did you tell Claude what you're
> doing?

>   MARGOT
>   (suddenly laughing)
> Jim, this guy, Malcolm. He's
> exactly what you'd imagine except I
> think he's clinically depressed.
>   (MORE)

MARGOT (CONT'D)
Not ugly, but completely unattractive. And he has no job. The best I can make out is that he's a letter writer. I don't know, the house looks weird to me...she's trying too hard and it's kind of a mess...they took down the swing...

Silence on the other end.

MARGOT
Hello?

JIM'S VOICE
You said you weren't a hundred percent on this. You said that like a week ago. Can I come up there?

MARGOT
No. I don't want to see you -- I feel happier already having done it.

JIM'S VOICE
Really? You feel happier...
    (silence)
Please don't tell Claude anything please, until we've talked more.

MARGOT
I need to tell him. And we need to tell Josh. Did he do his homework?

JIM'S VOICE
Yes.

MARGOT
This is happening and you have to get your mind around that.

15 INT. CLAUDE'S GUEST ROOM - NIGHT   15

Claude sleeps in bed. Margot gently touches his face. She whispers:

MARGOT
Are you asleep?

CLAUDE
    (softly)
Yes.

MARGOT
Will you remember this?

CLAUDE
Yes.

MARGOT
I just talked to your dad...

Claude's eyes remained closed, but he smiles.

MARGOT
I'm only going to tell you if you won't remember.

CLAUDE
Okay.

Margot hesitates. She changes her mind and says thoughtfully:

MARGOT
Everyone finds you so funny and charming. I always get compliments about you.

Margot stands. She catches herself in a warped mirror and smears some eye make-up off of her face.

MARGOT
Are you having fun? Is it nice to see Pauline?

CLAUDE
(opens his eyes)
Yeah, I really like her.

MARGOT
Yeah. She is crazy though.

CLAUDE
In what way?

MARGOT
She's really berserk. Maybe it's hormones. You don't notice anything different about Pauline?

CLAUDE
No.

                    MARGOT
          She's pregnant -- she told me. But
          she's keeping it a secret -- I mean
          from Malcolm and even Ingrid.
          Which I think is unforgiveable.
          Now she'll have to marry him.
          What's she planning -- to get
          married and not drink champagne?
          Then she'll just be lying. I guess
          she's afraid she'll miscarry. She
          probably will. I think on some
          level she's ambivalent about the
          marriage and that's why she's not
          telling him.

                    CLAUDE
          Are you stoned, Mom?

                    MARGOT
          Maybe a little.

                    CLAUDE
          I don't like it.

16   INT. MALCOLM AND PAULINE'S ROOM - NIGHT   16

Water runs from the bathroom. Malcolm cradles a glass of
whiskey and stands nude in front of a full length mirror.

                    MALCOLM
               (shakes his head)
          My scrotum is longer than my penis.

He turns around and looks at his ass. Pauline walks out of
the bathroom. She wears mens pajamas, the top open.

                    MALCOLM
          It's sweet how Claude looks up to
          me.

He waits for a reaction and gets none.

                    MALCOLM
          Margot doesn't seem as crazy as you
          made her out to be.

                    PAULINE
          What she did to Toby and Alan
          tonight didn't seem crazy enough
          for you?

                    MALCOLM
          I guess that seemed pretty crazy.

PAULINE
(immediately defensive)
Well, she cares deeply.

MALCOLM
Yeah, she's really worried about Bruce.

PAULINE
This has nothing to do with Bruce. She thinks everyone is autistic.

Malcolm is about to speak, but instead he halts, paralyzed.

PAULINE
What?

MALCOLM
Nothing, you keep changing your position -- I'm just trying to figure out if I should agree with you or not?

PAULINE
Well, can't she be both, care deeply <u>and</u> be crazy? Do people have to be all one thing?

MALCOLM
I guess not.

PAULINE
Well, okay...
(back into it)
It is nice she came for the wedding. She's so pretty, don't you think?

MALCOLM
(warily)
She's attractive.

PAULINE
A little thin maybe... But it is nice she came.

MALCOLM
Let's fuck.

17   INT. MARGOT'S GUEST ROOM - SAME   17

Margot lies on her front, her hand underneath her. She tries to masturbate. The bed creaks. Finally, she flips over and gives up. She wears a rubber night-guard in her mouth.

18   EXT. HOUSE - DAY   18

A croquet game in progress. Pauline and Malcolm play Margot and Claude. Ingrid lies in the grass singing to herself. The dog next to her. Malcolm concentrates -- he carefully lines up his shot. Finally, he swings --

The ball misses the wicket. He shakes with frustration.

                    MALCOLM
          Fuck it!

Claude looks through a slit in the wooden fence and into the neighbor's yard: A naked man, 40's, crouches. Arms extend from below and pull him downward. His ass pokes up over the weeds.

                    MARGOT
          Honey, you're up.

Claude shakes out of his reverie. He walks briskly up to his ball and smacks it. It bullets forward and lands just short of Pauline's ball.

                    MARGOT
          Claude, don't just whack it. Think
          about it before you hit.

                    CLAUDE
          Sorry.

Pauline knocks her ball into Claude's. She holds her ball down with her foot and prepares to swing.

                    MALCOLM
          Paul, what are you doing?

                    PAULINE
          I'm sending Claude's ball into the
          bushes.

                    MALCOLM
          Take the extra hit.

                    PAULINE
          I don't want to do that.

MALCOLM
It's the smarter play.

She whacks -- Claude's ball travels about two feet.

PAULINE
Shit.

MALCOLM
Pauline! See, I knew you
couldn't... Your feet are too
small!

Margot steps up to take her turn. She regards the house.

MARGOT
You took the awnings down.

Claude looks back into the adjacent yard: Flashes of skin. A breast. Pubic hair. Claude crouches to see more clearly -- the bodies disappear from sight.

Malcolm draws a deep breath and takes a few practice strokes. He swings -- his ball rockets past Margot's, rolls up over a ridge and onto the cement drive. It quickly sails down into the road and bounces into a ditch.

Malcolm shakes furiously. He lifts his mallet, turns toward the house, rethinks momentarily, and hurls it up over the incline and down to the water. Pauline puts her hands on her hips.

PAULINE
Well done.

MALCOLM
Fuck you.

Malcolm hesitates then tramps down the stairs to the beach.

Claude watches the pink of flesh moving up and down.

MARGOT
Honey, you're up.

He approaches his ball and smacks it toward the double wickets.

MARGOT
You're going the wrong way.

CLAUDE
Oh.

He blushes and laughs. Pauline laughs. Margot shakes her head.

                    MARGOT
          So stupid.

                    CLAUDE
          Mom, I'm sorry. Jesus.

Margot places her mallet down and starts toward the house.

                    CLAUDE
          We're in the middle of it.

                    MARGOT
          This is why I hate games. I hate
          what it does to me.

Pauline cackles loudly. Margot turns around and stares at her. Malcolm calls from the stairs:

                    MALCOLM (O.S.)
          Wait, we're not finished!

19   EXT. PATIO - DAY   19

The five eat a salad nicoise lunch.

                    MARGOT
          Malcolm, do you notice how Pauline
          sometimes can't make eye-contact.
          How her gaze hovers just above your
          head.

                    MALCOLM
          Yeah, I kind of know what you mean.

                    MARGOT
          I always think I have something in
          my hair. It's not necessarily bad,
          Paul. It's just something you do.

Pauline looks mildly horrified. She suddenly turns to Claude.

                    PAULINE
          Claude have you ever seen your
          mother climb a tree?

                    CLAUDE
          No.

                    MARGOT
          We don't have much opportunity in
          Manhattan.

                    PAULINE
          As kids Margot climbed everything.
          She could even climb that tree.

She points at the tall oak that stretches over the fence into
the neighbor's property.

                    CLAUDE
          Can you do it, mom?

                    MARGOT
          Maybe later.

                    CLAUDE
          No, now.

                    INGRID
          Do it now, Margot!

                    PAULINE
          Show him, Margot.

20   CUT TO: 20

Margot strides toward the tree. The group follows behind.

She grabs hold of a branch and lifts herself.

Claude grins, impressed.

With brisk dexterity, Margot scales the tree.

Claude, Pauline, Malcolm and Ingrid watch with glee from
below.

                    PAULINE
          I told you.

Margot reaches a perch near the top and looks down at the
gang. They wave. She waves back.

The sun is hot. She sweats, flushed. She takes a deep
breath and relaxes against the bark. Trees for miles. The
neighbors' house is faded and grey. In the far distance,
toxic white smoke comes out into the sky.

An earwig walks across her arm. She flicks it off, slips for
a moment and catches herself. Her breathing grows more
rapid.

A bug buzzes around her head. She swats at it.

Her family has stopped watching. Claude and Malcolm throw a baseball. Pauline's gone back inside. Ingrid clears the table.

                    MARGOT
            (under her breath)
  Shit.

She wipes her face, her shirt is almost entirely soaked. The buzzing continues.

Close on Margot's ear. A small black gnat lands on the lip of the lobe. It hesitates and darts inside the hole.

Margot gasps. She jams her pinky in her ear.

Pauline comes back out with an ice tea.

                    CLAUDE
  What's she doing now?

                    PAULINE
            (dryly)
  She's stuck.

21   CUT TO: 21

A young volunteer fireman climbs a long ladder up the side of the tree and toward Margot. He reaches out his hand to her.

                    MARGOT
            (annoyed)
  I got it.

She slowly lowers herself.

22   INT. LIVING ROOM - DAY   22

Pauline is laughing, recounting the story. Claude and Ingrid laugh too. Margot shakes her head, embarrassed and furious.

                    CLAUDE
  You were great on the way up.

                    MARGOT
  Don't patronize me, Claude.

Margot turns her head to the side and pats on the top of it.

                    PAULINE
  We're all laughing, Margot.

                    MARGOT
          You're laughing in a kind way.
          Claude is taking too much pleasure
          out of it.

                    CLAUDE
          I am not.

                    MARGOT
          You are. You like to make fun of
          me. To see me get embarrassed.
          It's mean.

Silence. Margot puts her pinky back in her ear. She frowns.

                    PAULINE
          What are you doing?

                    MARGOT
          I've got a fucking bug in my ear,
          okay?

23   EXT. FOREST - DAY   23

     Pauline and Margot hike along a dirt trail. Claude and
     Ingrid idle behind, carrying walking sticks.

                    PAULINE
          I thought Claude could hand out
          programs. Ingrid's going to sing.
          Do you want to read a poem or
          something?

                    MARGOT
          You know I can't speak in front of
          people. I'm doing this
          "conversation" at the bookstore in
          town on Friday and I totally regret
          having said I'd do it.

                    PAULINE
          You're doing a "conversation?"

                    MARGOT
          Yeah, talking about my work in
          front of a crowd. I didn't invite
          you because...I thought it'd be
          boring.

                    PAULINE
          Uh huh.

MARGOT
What? Say it.

PAULINE
It's nothing. It's just...I would come...I want to come. I get a kick out of it. It's just weird, you know... So, you're not here for...
    (she stops herself)
Okay, I get it. When did they ask you?

MARGOT
A while ago. I'd said, No, but then when I was coming here anyway and...I guess it helps sales and...so...so.

PAULINE
I see.

We catch a quick glimpse of people walking ahead in the path.

PAULINE
Did I tell you, Becky got her tubes tied.

MARGOT
Why? Is she seeing someone? She's still obese, I assume.

PAULINE
I think it's symbolic.

MARGOT
I bet mom paid for it. We should audit mom.

PAULINE
I considered it in my twenties. You know, when I was fucking everyone. You remember.

MARGOT
I did my share.

PAULINE
But not like me.

MARGOT
You want to count?

                    PAULINE
          No, Margot, I don't want to count.
               (pause)
          What was it about Dad that had us
          fucking so many guys?

                    MARGOT
          I think it was the only time we
          could really feel unselfconscious
          and get out of our heads.

                    PAULINE
               (dismissive)
          I don't think that's it. I just
          think it was something we were good
          at.

Behind, Ingrid smacks her walking stick into Claude's.

                    INGRID
          Your mom thinks Bruce is gay.

                    CLAUDE
          No, she said she had Aspergers.

                    INGRID
          I thought that's what that means.

                    CLAUDE
          No, it's like lesser retarded.

                    INGRID
          I have adult ADD.

                    CLAUDE
          You mean child ADD.

                    INGRID
          No, for some reason I have the
          adult one. Maybe I'm retarded.

Up ahead -- in the path -- is a couple, 40's, with a six year
old girl. The back of the man's pants are smeared with dirt
and the woman is packed into acid washed jeans. The little
girl whines and lags behind.

Margot and Pauline slow down. Claude and Ingrid catch up.

                    MAN
          Come on!

                    LITTLE GIRL
          I don't want to!

                    MAN
          Come on!

                    LITTLE GIRL
          I don't want --

The woman grabs the girl harshly by the arm and pulls her.
The girl screams.

                    MARGOT
          Hey!

The man and woman turn around sharply.

                    MARGOT
          Be careful!

                    WOMAN
          What?

                    MARGOT
          Be careful the way you pull on that
          child's arm. You'll take it out of
          its socket.

                    MAN
          Don't tell us how to treat our
          child.

                    MARGOT
          I don't care how you treat your
          child as long as you don't hurt
          him.

                    PAULINE
             (under her breath)
          It's a girl.

                    WOMAN
          She threw a rock at me.

                    MARGOT
          She's a little girl!

                    WOMAN
          She knew what she was doing.

She starts suddenly toward Margot.

                    WOMAN
          There is no hitting in our family.
          Do you understand?

Margot backs up quickly. The woman stops about ten feet away.

                WOMAN
    Stay out of it, bitch.

The woman turns back around. She lifts the girl into her arms and they trudge over the incline and out of sight.

                INGRID
    That was the Voglers.

                PAULINE
    Jesus, Margot, what are you doing.
    They already hate us.

                MARGOT
      (wiping her eyes)
    Don't tell me what I can and can't
    do. That's child abuse.

                CLAUDE
    Mom, she was psychotic.

                MARGOT
    Stop picking on me. Everyone.

24   CUT TO: 24

The four of them emerge into a clearing. Nobody speaks. A child's pink sneaker lies in the path.

                MARGOT
    Oh God.

Pauline walks over to it. She crouches.

                PAULINE
    It could be anyone's.

Margot bursts into tears. Pauline hesitates then holds her.

                INGRID
    What are they going to do to us?

                PAULINE
    They're not going to do anything,
    honey.

25   EXT. FRONT PORCH - DAY   25

Malcolm looks at Pauline. He's in the midst of writing a letter on a legal pad. Pauline is worked up.

PAULINE
We have to cut down that tree.

MALCOLM
Where are we going to get married
then?

PAULINE
I don't...we'll do it in the
fucking drive-way if we have to.

Claude and Ingrid listen from just inside the house. Ingrid
looks at Claude nervously.

INGRID
Your mom started a war. We have to
make sure we wear shoes because
they might start throwing glass.

CLAUDE
Has that happened before?

INGRID
I can't remember. I think so. No,
it definitely has. Now I remember.

Behind them, Margot, made-up and wearing a dress, clomps down
the stairs, across the carpet and onto the porch.

PAULINE
Where are you going?

MARGOT
(tersely)
To town. I'll be back for dinner.

PAULINE
Come on, nobody blames you, Margot.

An old orange BMW idles at the end of the driveway. Pauline,
Malcolm, Claude and Ingrid watch Margot cross the drive-way.

A man, 50's, opens the passenger door. He smokes a brown
cigarette. Margot gets in. The man waves at the group on
the patio. Pauline, Malcolm and Ingrid and Claude wave back.

CLAUDE
Is that Dick Koosman?

PAULINE
Yeah. He has a house up here.

                    CLAUDE
          What's he doing with mom?

                    PAULINE
          Good question.

26   EXT. HOUSE - DAY   26

     Ingrid sits at the roots of the tree, squeezing honey out of
     a honey bear onto her hand -- she watches the ants come.
     Claude sits on a low branch and looks over the fence:

                    INGRID
          How much do your parents make in a
          year?

                    CLAUDE
          I think about a hundred. They bank
          at Chase.

     The front door of the Vogler's opens and a boy, 14, pees from
     the entrance-way into the plants in the yard.

                    INGRID
          Are they rich?

                    CLAUDE
          No. They're middle class.

     The boy finishes and violently hurls a toy car at the fence.

                    BOY
          Just let me live!

     The toy lands a few feet short. He goes inside and closes
     the door.

                    INGRID
          Upper or lower?

                    CLAUDE
          I think just middle.

     Claude watches: Malcolm scurries around the side of the
     Vogler house holding a dead mole by its tail. He stumbles,
     recovers and flings the animal at the front door. He races
     back toward his property.

27   EXT. PORCH - EVENING   27

     Margot and Malcolm have cocktails. Pauline drinks a bottled
     water. Ingrid has cray pas, markers and paper and draws at a
     table. She draws a mole.

Claude draws a boy with a big claw for a hand and CLAWED under it. Wizard, the dog, lies at his feet.

> MARGOT
> Dick and his daughter asked us over to swim tomorrow.

> PAULINE
> We didn't invite them to the wedding.

> MARGOT
> You're not really friends.

> PAULINE
> We're friends enough that's it's awkward. Maisy baby-sits for us all the time.

> MARGOT
> He's doing the interview with me in town on Friday. Did I tell you, he and I are collaborating on a screenplay, an adaptation of one of Dick's novels.

> PAULINE
> No, I didn't even know you knew he was up here.

Malcolm takes one of Ingrid's markers and doodles.

> MALCOLM
> Is he even a good writer? Why do people care about him?

> PAULINE
> You're competitive with everyone. It doesn't matter if they even do the same thing as you.
>   (to Claude)
> He's competitive with Bono.

> MALCOLM
> It's true. I don't subscribe to the credo that there's enough room for everyone to be successful. I think there are only a few spots available and people like Dick Koosman and Bono are taking them up.

Pauline looks at Malcolm's drawing. It's a graphic image of a man fucking a woman in the ass.

                    PAULINE
          Malcolm, what would ever make you
          think that's something to draw
          right now?

Claude and Ingrid stare at it. Malcolm balls it up.

                    MALCOLM
          Sorry, I wasn't thinking about it.
          Sorry, Margot.

28   INT. VOLVO - DAY   28

The car pulls into a driveway. A modern house. Dick and
Maisy come out to greet them.

                    DICK
          You found it!

Margot, the kids and Pauline get out. We stay in the car
with Malcolm. Pauline comes to his window.

                    PAULINE
          What's up?

                    MALCOLM
          I don't want to do this...

                    PAULINE
          Come on, don't be that way.

Maisy sits on the hood of the car and Ingrid introduces her
to Claude. Dick approaches Margot -- she turns back to
Pauline.

                    MALCOLM
          I'm not being that way -- I just
          don't feel like it. I'm going to
          go back and... I have work to do.

                    PAULINE
          Dick doesn't care that you don't
          make any money.

                    MALCOLM
          Is that why you think... That's
          not why I'm...I just hate swimming.
          I really hate it. It's disgusting
          to me. My mistake was saying I'd
          do it to begin with. You have fun.

                    PAULINE
          Fine, we'll have fun.

Malcolm's gaze goes to Maisy's breasts. Margot watches him watch her.

                    MALCOLM
          People always pee in the pool.

                    PAULINE
          I don't think Dick and Maisy pee in
          their pool.

                    MALCOLM
          I'll bet you 500 dollars there's
          pee in that pool.

29   EXT. DICK'S POOL - DAY   29

Pauline and Margot float beneath Claude who stands above them.

                    PAULINE
          To the end and back. Claude, you
          say Go.

                    CLAUDE
          Okay.

Margot knocks on the side of her head with her hand.

                    CLAUDE
          Go!

Pauline flings herself in and is off. Margot hesitates then follows. Maisy and Dick watch from the chairs. Ingrid floats on a raft and cheers. Claude runs along the pool-side.

                    DICK
          How's your dad?

                    CLAUDE
          Good.

                    DICK
          He and I shared a thesis advisor at
          Stanford. Did you know that?

                    CLAUDE
          No.

Pauline hits the far wall with her palm and flips around. Margot stops short and follows her sister. They're neck and neck. Their arms cut in and out of the water.

                    DICK
          I was dating your mom back then,
          did you know that?

                    CLAUDE
          No.

Pauline lands -- touches the wall first. Margot a close second.

                    CLAUDE
          Pauline wins!

Pauline beams. Margot immediately drifts to the ladder. She's panting heavily.

                    CLAUDE
          Mom cheated. You didn't touch the
          wall!

                    MARGOT
          I did so. It doesn't matter. I
          lost anyway.

                    PAULINE
          It was close.

Pauline floats on her back, exhausted.

Ingrid swims beneath Claude -- long strands of hair stream up from beneath the surface.

Margot gets out of the water and Dick wraps her in a towel. For a moment it's an embrace. Margot looks quickly over at Claude --

His foot slips.

He topples in.

Water roars around him.

He opens his mouth. Bubbles spurt out.

He drifts down.

Lying next to the drain is a field mouse. Its eyes are white.

Splash. Hands wrap around him.

He goes up.

The sounds of wind and blurry voices now clearer.

Pauline brings Claude to the surface and pushes him to the ladder. She helps him climb out. Ingrid and Maisy are grinning. Their expressions slowly shift as they see Claude's face.

Claude is sobbing.

                  PAULINE
     It's okay.

Margot immediately wrenches Claude from Pauline's grasp. She looks shocked and angry.

                  MARGOT
     I got him.

She leads her son behind the bushes out of everyone's sight.

                  MARGOT
     It's okay, my baby.

She gently lets him down. His sneakers squeak and slosh. Claude, soaking wet and ashamed, looks at his mother. She breaks into laughter. Claude wipes the water and tears from his eyes.

                  CLAUDE
     I'm sorry I laughed about the tree.

                  MARGOT
     Now we're even.

30   INT. PAULINE AND MALCOLM'S DEN - DAY   30

Margot, reclining on the couch, drinks a white wine with ice cubes. Pauline passes the doorway and stops. She holds tear-sheets of flowers and wedding decorations from various magazines.

                  PAULINE
     Here you are.

                  MARGOT
     You've got a problem.

                  PAULINE
     What do you mean?

                  MARGOT
     I don't like the girl and I don't
     like the way Malcolm looks at her.

                    PAULINE
          Oh, come on, it's sexy.

                    MARGOT
          You didn't see it. I saw it.
          You've got a problem.

                    PAULINE
          I'm not worried.
               (pause)
          We could teach Claude how to swim.

                    MARGOT
          He won't want to do it. It's too
          late.

Pauline waits for more -- nothing comes. She takes a couple
steps into the room. She holds out her hand for the glass.
Margot passes it to her. Pauline sips.

                    MARGOT
          Are you supposed to be doing that?

                    PAULINE
          No.

She hands it back.

                    PAULINE
          I liked your last story in, was it
          Harpers? The one about mom. I was
          very...I liked it very much.

                    MARGOT
          It wasn't really about mom.

                    PAULINE
          I thought it was. Anyway. Why
          don't you want Claude to know how
          to swim?

                    MARGOT
          I didn't say I didn't want him to.
          Why do you care? It's not in his
          life -- we're New Yorkers. If he
          wants to learn when he's older, he
          can. I'm curious why you're so
          interested in the whole thing.

                    PAULINE
          I'm not. I'm just... As a safety
          thing and...I'm... Forget it.
               (pause)
                                     (MORE)

                    PAULINE (CONT'D)
          It's interesting -- this is the
          first time Dick has invited us
          over.

                    MARGOT
          But are you really friends?

                    PAULINE
          Kind of. We're neighbors. We
          employ Maisy. I mean I don't care,
          I just think it's interesting.
               (pause)
          Are you excited about the talk? I
          thought I'd come if that's okay.
          My friend, Agnes, asked me, "What's
          it like to have a celebrity as a
          sister?" I said, I've got no
          problem with celebrity. Alice
          Munro taught at Bennington and was
          kind of a friend of mine.

                    MARGOT
          I'm not a celebrity.

                    PAULINE
          Well, you're well known.

                    MARGOT
          To a very few people.

                    PAULINE
          Just accept the compliment.

                    MARGOT
          I guess I didn't realize it was a
          compliment.

31   EXT. FOREST - LATE DAY   31

Margot walks the path alone. She hugs herself as a light
breeze kicks up. Her footsteps echo in the trees.

The little pink sneaker still lies in the dirt.

She crouches down and takes it.

32   CUT TO: 32

CLOSE: A note is being written.

"...and if you are acting with any sort of abuse toward your
child I will call the police."

The word "any" is then underlined twice. The page is torn from her little brown book.

33   EXT. VOGLER HOUSE - EVENING   33

Margot's fist is raised about to knock on the front door. She stops herself. She puts the note on the Welcome mat and holds it in place with the child's shoe. She wanders around to the back of the house. She looks into a lighted window:

It's a white tiled bathroom.

A wet brown animal body covered in clear plastic is balanced on the sink. Mr. Vogler tears into the plastic. The carcass is butterflied open exposing the innards and ribs.

Mrs. Vogler runs the tub. She pours salt from a box in the water. The man slides his hand in her waist-band. She rubs against him.

Margot chews her cuticle.

The man saws the legs. His arm jerks back and forth, straining to cut through the bone. Sweat pours down his temples.

Margot raises her hand to her face and presses against the window. She peers through her fingers. The blade pierces the bone with a violent release and the hoof falls to the floor.

Margot moves to another window. The pig's face now looks at her.

Blood drips and leaks into the crevices of the tile. The woman brandishes a syringe filled with an orange liquid.

Suddenly a face appears in the glass. Margot leaps back. It's a thin boy. He says something. The family turns to the window. The father flicks off the bathroom light.

From inside Margot illuminates like an apparition.

Margot scampers into the trees. She pushes through branches, her shirt tears. She runs.

34   INT. CLAUDE'S GUEST ROOM - EVENING   34

Claude sits on the bed. The record sleeve from Blondie's "Parallel Lines" rests in his lap. He reads the lyrics to the song, "Sunday Girl." He depresses the red record button on an old portable tape recorder. He sings a cappella and full voice, passionately, as sweetly as he can.

Maisy appears in the doorway and watches. Claude turns mid-lyric. He jumps, startled.

                    MAISY
          Singing?

Fumbling, Claude shuts off the tape recorder.

                    CLAUDE
          Hm? A bit.

She drifts into the room and hovers closely above Claude who remains on the bed.

Margot passes by in the hallway, disheveled from her escape. She watches: Maisy takes the lyric sleeve from Claude's hands. Her T-shirt hangs above her waist showing her smooth stomach.

                    MAISY
          Can I make a suggestion?

                    CLAUDE
          Uh huh.

                    MAISY
          You should get underarm deodorant.

                    CLAUDE
          Uh huh.

                    MAISY
          You kind of smell.

Claude blushes.

                    MAISY
          Better I tell you than someone
          else.

35   INT. MARGOT'S BATHROOM - EVENING   35

Margot puts on mascara and watches Claude, who stands behind her, in the mirror.

                    MARGOT
          I think you smell nice. You smell
          real.

                    CLAUDE
          I stink.

MARGOT
It causes cancer.

CLAUDE
Underarm deodorant?

MARGOT
Yes. It's got chemicals and things that are extremely harmful.

CLAUDE
I'm not going to die from underarm cancer.

MARGOT
No, you'll get it somewhere else. Like your stomach or your testicles.

CLAUDE
(laughs)
Testicles.

MARGOT
Don't laugh, that's a serious thing.
Who told you this, anyway? Maisy?

CLAUDE
Yeah.

MARGOT
I hope you're not interested in that girl. I find her insufferable.

CLAUDE
What does that mean?

MARGOT
It means I can't suffer her. She's loud and stupid. She goes on about things of which she knows nothing about.

CLAUDE
She got into Harvard early.

MARGOT
Stupid people get into Harvard early all the time.

CLAUDE
Where did you go again?

MARGOT
Barnard.
(pause)
I just don't think you should do anything with her.

CLAUDE
(embarrassed)
We're just friends.

MARGOT
If you do, use a condom.

Claude looks into the toilet. A square of toilet paper with a red lip outline floats on top of the water.

CLAUDE
Where are you going?

MARGOT
Out with Paul and Malcolm and Dick.

CLAUDE
Are kids coming?

36 INT. LIVING ROOM - NIGHT   36

Claude's POV through the window: Dick and Margot in the back seat of the Volvo. Malcolm and Pauline the front. The ignition turns.

Claude leaves the window. We hear the car rumble away. Claude and Ingrid sit on the couch, hamburgers in front of them. Maisy is cross-legged on Wizard's dog bed and chews a stalk of celery.

INGRID
Who do we know who's gay?

MAISY
How do I know what gay people you know.

CLAUDE
Alan and Toby.

INGRID
And Bruce. He's gay and Aspergers.

CLAUDE
I don't know if Bruce is gay.

INGRID
He might be, it's very common.

CLAUDE
Your mom is pregnant.

INGRID
No she isn't.

CLAUDE
She is.

Ingrid looks stricken.

MAISY
How do you know that, Claude?

CLAUDE
She told my mom. But you can tell -- she's hormonally weird.

MAISY
Holy shit, Ingrid you're going to have a baby sister or brother.

INGRID
(quietly)
My mom thinks your mom is unreliable.

CLAUDE
Who cares.

But he does. Claude bites into his burger. His eyes fix on the crease between Maisy's breasts. Maisy says to Claude:

MAISY
Do you think your mom is fuckable?

CLAUDE
I don't know.

MAISY
I think she's hot, your mother. I'd do her if I was gay. I might anyway. I mean if she came on to me.

CLAUDE
She won't.

                    INGRID
          I'm not going to do anyone.

There's a scraping sound on the window. The kids turn
quickly:

                    CLAUDE
          What was that?

                    INGRID
          Is it scary?

37   EXT. FIELD - NIGHT   37

The three kids lie in the grass and watch through the slats
in the fence: The Vogler family eats at an outdoor table. A
pig turns on a spit over a smoky barbecue. Mrs. Vogler says
something and the kids and Mr. Vogler laugh.

Maisy climbs over Claude to see better. He feels her breasts
press against his back. Suddenly he swats crazily at his
ear. Ingrid is poking him with a blade of grass.

38   INT. VOLVO - NIGHT   38

Malcolm drives quickly with Pauline next to him. He's
smoking with the window open, Dick and Margot in the
backseat.

                    PAULINE
          Margot used to never speak. I
          remember when we went on a double
          date in high school, that kid Ron
          asked you if English was your first
          language.

                    MARGOT
          It's true. I used to think I might
          have some kind of brain defect.

                    PAULINE
          You thought you were aphasic.

                    MARGOT
          I'm still not sure.

                    PAULINE
          Oh, Jesus, Margot.

                    MARGOT
          It's very possible, Paul.

PAULINE
I just...your diagnoses sometimes
irk the hell out of me.

Malcolm lights another cigarette -- the car jerks sideways.

MARGOT
Malcolm, can you slow down.

MALCOLM
What?

DICK
I can drive if you like.

MALCOLM
No, you got dinner, the driving's
on me.

DICK
Well, I'll let you pay your half if
you'll slow down.

MALCOLM
Well, neither Pauline or I ordered
dessert.

PAULINE
Malcolm, let it go.
    (taunting)
Margot would insist on driving if
she knew how.

MARGOT
    (to Dick)
My license elapsed. But I know
how.

MALCOLM
It's probably for the best. I have
this theory, I think, historically,
women have been held back in so
many ways that when they get power,
like they do behind the wheel, they
can't help but abuse it. It's akin
to Hannah Arendt's Eichmann theory
about prison guards and prisoners
switching rolls.

DICK
That's a charming philosophy.

MARGOT
Yeah. Tell that one a lot.

MALCOLM
This isn't a blanket thing. I mean, women can be great drivers too...

He takes a long satisfied drag on his cigarette.

PAULINE
Said the man with the moustache that he thinks he's wearing in quotes.

MARGOT
It's meant to be funny.

MALCOLM
(to Pauline, re: Margot)
Are you doing this for her benefit or mine?

Malcolm pumps the brake.

MALCOLM
What the fuck?

PAULINE
What?

MALCOLM
(momentarily sober)
No, there they go. Okay. It's fine. I thought I had no brakes for a minute...

Malcolm pitches his cigarette out the window -- it flies through Margot's window and lands on her lap.

MARGOT
Malcolm!

Dick grabs the lit butt and chucks it in the road.

MALCOLM
(turning around)
What?!

The car swerves again -- everyone jumps.

MARGOT
Watch it!

                    MALCOLM
          It's fine, Margot!

                    PAULINE
              (to Malcolm)
          You're just so incompetent.

                    MALCOLM
              (exploding)
          Why don't you fucking drive
          yourselves home!

Malcolm screeches the vehicle over to the shoulder. They
jolt to a stop.

                    PAULINE
              (quietly furious)
          Oh, God.

Pauline opens the door and staggers toward the brush. She
leans against a tree and looks like she might vomit. Malcolm
watches in the rearview mirror.

                    MARGOT
          You should go after her.

Malcolm sighs heavily and gets out of the car. Margot and
Dick watch out the back window. Pauline sees Malcolm coming
and bolts into the woods. Malcolm charges after her.

                    DICK
          Come back with me tonight.

                    MARGOT
          I've got Claude.

                    DICK
          Come on, I've been trying to get
          you up here all year.

                    MARGOT
              (vaguely)
          She's pregnant.

Dick leans over to Margot's neck. He licks her.

39   INT. INGRID'S ROOM - NIGHT   39

Claude lies in bed with Ingrid. He chews off a piece of his
pinky fingernail. He hesitates and places it on an end-
table.

INGRID
Why are you putting that there?

CLAUDE
I just want to keep it.

INGRID
I left a piece of skin in a movie theater once so it could watch movies all its life.

CLAUDE
I don't know if it's the same thing.

INGRID
Are you obsessed with Maisy?

CLAUDE
No.

INGRID
You're always staring at her tits.

Ingrid traces Claude's upper lip with her finger.

INGRID
You have a moustache.

CLAUDE
My mom bleaches it.

INGRID
I'm going to kiss your cheek and then you kiss mine.

CLAUDE
I don't want to do that.

INGRID
Why not?

CLAUDE
Because it's pointless...

Claude hears footsteps creak downstairs. He goes to the door and peers out: Pauline and Malcolm, a little disheveled and dirty, climb the stairs. Neither speaks. Malcolm goes into the hall bathroom. Pauline into their room. Running water groans through the old pipes.

                    INGRID
          Where are you going? I thought we
          were having a conversation.

                    CLAUDE
          You're starting to annoy me.

40   INT. HALLWAY - CONTINUOUS   40

     Claude walks -- he passes an open door: Malcolm is shaving
     his moustache -- the electric razor whirring.

41   INT. MARGOT'S ROOM - CONTINUOUS   41

     Claude enters. It's empty. Her brown notebook rests on the
     bedside table. He hesitates then opens it:

     It's packed with writing -- a nearly indecipherable cursive
     in black ink. The name Claude can be made out on the page.

     Claude takes the book and climbs up into bed. He nestles
     against the pillow and squints to read the writing.

                    MARGOT (O.S.)
          What are you doing?

     Claude startles. Margot stands in the doorway with a glass
     of water.

                    CLAUDE
          I didn't think you came home.

                    MARGOT
          Where would I be?

                    CLAUDE
          Can't Josh and Dad come to the
          wedding?

                    MARGOT
          We've been through this. Go to
          bed.

     Claude slides down to the floor. He hesitates.

                    CLAUDE
          Can I sleep in here?

                    MARGOT
          No, honey.

                    CLAUDE
          We can put a pillow between us.

                    MARGOT
          Okay. Just for tonight.

Claude takes a long pillow and places it like a barrier in
the bed. We stay on him as he waits. Finally Margot climbs
into the covers in a nightgown.

                    MARGOT
          When you were a baby I wouldn't let
          anyone else hold you. I think that
          may have been a mistake.

42   EXT. HOUSE - MORNING   42

Malcolm, his moustache gone, a cigarette dangling from his
mouth, hammers in a stake at the base of a collapsed, white
tent. A workman holds a pole steadily.

Pauline sets up chairs around a series of tables. Ingrid
idles a few feet away. They're in the midst of talking:

                    INGRID
          Why was it a secret?

                    PAULINE
          Because I didn't want to get you
          excited before it was real. It's
          not really a baby yet. In two more
          weeks we can celebrate together,
          okay?

                    INGRID
          Why did you tell Margot?

                    PAULINE
          Because she's my sister and I trust
          her. How do you feel about it?

                    INGRID
          I don't want a sister.

Pauline touches Ingrid's hair gently.

                    INGRID
          I'm going to go get Wizard.

She runs toward the house. Pauline marches toward Malcolm.

                    PAULINE
          Margot told Claude something I
          expressly told her in confidence.
          And he told Ingrid.
                    (MORE)

PAULINE (CONT'D)
I'm stunned that she put me in this position. It's so fucking infuriating.

MALCOLM
Well it's that thing where--

PAULINE
Don't say anything. You know what...just be there for me. Silently.

MALCOLM
Okay.

PAULINE
Why do I have to be so careful around her, but everyone is allowed to make fun of me?

MALCOLM
I don't know if --

PAULINE
Malcolm, what did I just say?
    (sighs)
You know, I just want you to take my side, I don't need you to make it better.

Malcolm puts his hand awkwardly on her shoulder.

PAULINE
Ingrid's really upset about it. Fuck. I can't **believe** she did this to me!
    (pause)
I didn't tell you because... I didn't want you to feel like you had to marry me. I found out right before our seminar... I'm pregnant.

MALCOLM
Uh huh.

PAULINE
Well...does that sound good to you?

MALCOLM
I'm still digesting Margot telling Claude. What a fucking nut job.
    (quickly)
Sorry. I think I'm really happy.

Ingrid is watching from across the field.

> PAULINE
> Come here, honey!

Ingrid hurries through the sparkly, dewy grass. Pauline hugs her and they spin.

CUT TO:

Margot watches from the upstairs window. The mother and daughter walk arm in arm down what will be the aisle. Finally, Margot turns away -- she's in Pauline and Malcolm's room.

She opens drawers: Underwear, socks, bras. Topless photos of Pauline posing in the bedroom. A photograph of Margot and Pauline in their teens on Halloween dressed as Pat Benatar and Patty Smyth respectively.

Margot grins.

Another photo of Margot, Pauline and an obese woman -- Becky -- in their 20's.

Margot's expression saddens. She opens another drawer. Polaroids of Pauline and Malcolm in different sexual poses.

She flips through these and drops them on the bureau.

Amidst the underwear and socks she finds pill containers. She squints to read the labels. She opens one and shakes out a few blue pills into her palm. She swallows one and puts the rest in her pocket.

More drawers open: Self-help books, incense, pamphlets on Buddhism. A stack of pornographic DVD's.

> CLAUDE (O.S.)
> Hey.

Margot starts and shoves the drawer shut.

> MARGOT
> Hey. I'm just looking at Pauline's incense and self-help books. I don't understand it. This junk makes her look stupid and she's not. I don't like to think of her this way.

> CLAUDE
> Uh huh.

                    MARGOT
          She's such a hypocrite. Somehow
          I'm a kook for going to therapy,
          but she's got enough drugs here to
          medicate a...
              (settles on a word)
          ...an elephant. And she's always
          with these losers.

                    CLAUDE
          Malcolm's not a loser.

                    MARGOT
          Claude...think about it.

                    CLAUDE
          He's cool.

                    MARGOT
          What makes you think he's cool?
              (softens)
          I'm more talking about her
          investment in things like the Forum
          and ashrams.

                    CLAUDE
          What's the Forum?

                    MARGOT
          Like a cult.

                    CLAUDE
          She was in a cult?

                    MARGOT
          Years ago. She and Lenny also
          followed some guru who was a
          follower of the Mukdananda who made
          her drink his bath water. Who
          knows what she's doing now.

                    INGRID (O.S.)
          Margot! Claude!

44   EXT. FIELD - DAY   44

       Claude hacks his way through the tall weeds.

                    CLAUDE
          Wizard!

       We move past him, obscured by grass, Pauline and Ingrid yell:

                    PAULINE/INGRID
              Wizard! Wiz!

Margot enters the frame. The kids walk ahead.

                    MARGOT
              Wizard! Here, boy!

She stands a few feet away from Pauline. The kids can be
heard shouting in the distance.

                    MARGOT
              How long has he been gone?

                    PAULINE
              I don't know. Ingrid brought him
              in last night, but we couldn't find
              him this morning.

                    MARGOT
              Oh boy.

                    PAULINE
              Did you tell Claude I'm pregnant?

                    MARGOT
              I don't know.

                    PAULINE
              You did.

                    MARGOT
              I guess I said something.

                    PAULINE
              You did. You don't have to tell
              him everything.

                    MARGOT
              He wants to know. If I don't tell
              him, he figures it out.

                    INGRID (O.S.)
              Where is Wizard?

Ingrid approaches with Claude.

                    PAULINE
              I don't know, honey.

Ingrid sinks into her mother's body. Claude and Margot walk
ahead.

                        CLAUDE
            You didn't let him go out into the
            road or something where something
            could've happened to him?

                        MARGOT
            Why would you think I'd do
            something like that? That's awful.

                        CLAUDE
            I just... I'm just making sure.

                        MARGOT
            That's a terrible thing to say to
            me.

                        CLAUDE
            I didn't mean on purpose, I just
            meant maybe in case...you knew
            something. I'm sorry.

45   INT. KITCHEN - DAY   45

        Margot enters and opens the refrigerator. She gets out a
        white wine bottle. She turns around and jumps, startled.

                        MARGOT
            Woa!

        Malcolm sits at the table, eating saltines out of the box, a
        pad and paper in front of him.

                        MALCOLM
            Hey, sorry. I'm here.

                        MARGOT
            No, I... I should've looked.

                        MALCOLM
            I'm just writing my vows. Trying
            to do something appropriate but
            also funny -- not jokey, more
            character based humor.

        Margot pours herself a glass of wine. She looks to Malcolm
        to see if he wants some. He shakes his head. She takes a
        long drink. Silence.

                        MALCOLM
            You having an okay time?

                        MARGOT
            Oh, yeah. Besides Wizard getting --

MALCOLM
Yeah, we'll...we'll find him...or else, I don't know...

MARGOT
We won't.

MALCOLM
Right, or else he's dead or something.
    (pause)
It means a lot to Paul that you came.

MARGOT
Yeah.

Silence. Malcolm mumbles a tune.

MARGOT
Oh God, this is the same toaster we had here as kids. Paul is so weird.

MALCOLM
I hear you've heard the news.

MARGOT
Yeah. Congratulations.

MALCOLM
Pretty cool. Hard to fully take in. It's a little abstract still. I haven't had that thing yet where you realize that you're not the most important person in the world. I'm anxious for that to happen. I guess I have to thank you -- I wouldn't know yet if you hadn't arrived.

MARGOT
You're welcome.

MALCOLM
Of course I can't help but worry I'll pass some not so great genes onto the kid. I mean, in my family there's a lot of hand washing, you know. I don't have it, but my brother does.
    (pause)
You working on anything now?

MARGOT
Besides the thing with Dick?

MALCOLM
Oh, right.

He nods. She nods. Silence.

MARGOT
How about you?

MALCOLM
Oh, I'm working on some acrylic paint --

MARGOT
Nobody fills the ice cube trays.

Malcolm stops, immediately embarrassed. Margot is looking in the freezer. She takes out the trays and brings them to the sink. She runs the water.

MARGOT
Sorry, what were you --

MALCOLM
Nothing. It doesn't matter.

MARGOT
No, what were you saying?

MALCOLM
It really... Nothing.

MARGOT
Okay.

She treads back to the refrigerator, balancing the full trays.

MALCOLM
I was saying I'm doing these abstractions in acrylic paint. But it's not... I'm not getting paid or anything. I don't know, I hate that question, "What do you do?"

MARGOT
You asked me.

MALCOLM
I know, but...

Malcolm exhales in frustration.

46   EXT. FIELD - DAY   46

Pauline and Malcolm open the gate to the Vogler's property.

> MALCOLM
> I think we shouldn't mention the tree, we should let them know that there will be people and music on Saturday and it will be louder than usual.

> PAULINE
> And that they can come for a glass of champagne. But you tell them. I think they respond to you better.

They approach the Vogler's sun-worn and paint chipped house.

> MALCOLM
> Well, I am ultimately one of them. You shouldn't've made me shave the stache.

> PAULINE
> (laughs)
> Yeah, right.

> MALCOLM
> Oh, hey, Ingrid is asking me if I was ever gay. Do you know what that's about?

> PAULINE
> No.

Mr. Vogler, wearing a fleece vest and carrying a hatchet over his shoulders, tramples out of the brush.

> PAULINE
> Hi.

Vogler stops. His face is jagged and worn.

> PAULINE
> Hi, I'm Pauline. This is Malcolm. We've met before. We're your neighbors.

The man watches them strangely with icy blue eyes.

                        VOGLER
              You gonna cut that tree down?

                        PAULINE
              Well, we grew up with that tree and
              we're getting married under it
              Saturday and --

She waits for Malcolm to jump in. He doesn't. Vogler says
softly, but sternly:

                        VOGLER
              The roots are growing into our
              property. It's rotting, it's
              killing our plants.

                        PAULINE
              We had a tree doctor out and he
              said it was healthy.

Pauline smacks Malcolm's arm.

                        PAULINE
              Would it hurt you to say anything?

                        MALCOLM
              What? What do you want from me?

                        PAULINE
              You're making me do the whole
              fucking thing.

                        MALCOLM
              You brought up the tree.

                        PAULINE
              He brought up --

She stops herself. She says to Vogler:

                        PAULINE
              I'm sorry... This was better
              thought-through back at the house.

Pauline's gaze goes above Vogler's head -- like Margot
described earlier. He runs his hand through his hair as if
something might be caught in there.

                        PAULINE
              We were wondering if you and your
              wife -- I'm sorry I forgot her name
              -- would like to come over for...

VOGLER
You should ask her. She makes the plans. I'm going to go in now.

He tramps inside. The screen door bangs.

MALCOLM
I felt like you didn't give me a chance to say what I wanted to say.

Pauline hits him in the chest and starts to walk away. Malcolm comes after her, his rage growing.

MALCOLM
I want to punch that guy in the nose!

PAULINE
You've never hit anyone.

MALCOLM
I have too!

PAULINE
Who?

MALCOLM
Lots of -- You don't know them. They're not around because I've punched them.

A smile breaks across Pauline's face. Malcolm seethes.

MALCOLM
Don't laugh, Pauline. It's not funny. I'll fucking punch your sister.

Malcolm clenches his fists. He points at Vogler's place.

MALCOLM
The threat is not out there. It's in <u>our</u> house. It's sleeping in my studio. I mean, I wouldn't actually hit her, but I feel...I feel like doing it. She's such a fucking idiot.

PAULINE
She's not an idiot. You might not like her --

MALCOLM
She is. She is an idiot! You're an idiot.

PAULINE
Jesus.

MALCOLM
You're both fucking morons. I'm so fucking... I'm trying so hard. You don't give me any credit.

PAULINE
What is wrong?

MALCOLM
I don't know, I have the emotional version of whatever bad feng shui would be. I don't know. You tell me, you understand this shit.

PAULINE
Did you drink your teas?

MALCOLM
Yeah, I drank my fucking teas! Don't judge me now. Really, I think when you look back at this you're going to see I'm not acting like a crazy person. That this is the right reaction. In proportion with what is going on. This is right!

Malcolm looks around furiously. The only thing available to him is a leafy stalk. He pulls on it, but it won't uproot. He tears the leaves off in a rage.

PAULINE
You have the most oddly self-conscious form of rage I've ever --

MALCOLM
I hate you.

Exhausted he approaches her. He says, still with anger:

MALCOLM
Let's make love.

47   CUT TO: 47

Pauline walks back to the house, buttoning her dress. She
looks up suddenly and stops: A man watches her from the lawn.
He holds a bouquet of flowers. Pauline runs to him.

                    PAULINE
          Jim...

They embrace. Her hand cups the back of his neck.

                    CLAUDE (O.S.)
          Dad!

Claude runs from the house.

48   EXT. PATIO - LATE DAY   48

Pauline, Malcolm, Margot, Jim, Claude and Ingrid eat fish
stew and peasant bread. Jim's flowers sit in a vase. He
wears a tan knit bracelet that Ingrid made.

                    JIM
          It was a difficult decision because
          Claude has so many friends at
          school now, but it is expensive and
          Bronx Science is a great public
          school.

                    CLAUDE
          I didn't get into Stuyvesant.

                    MARGOT
          He's not a good test taker.

                    MALCOLM
          I went to Stuy.

                    MARGOT
               (caught off-guard)
          Really?

                    MALCOLM
          Really.

                    CLAUDE
          I'd rather stay at Packer, but it's
          so expensive.

Malcolm lifts up a bottle of Jameson from the floor near his
chair and pours himself another stiff drink.

JIM
Josh is a great test taker, but Claude thinks more abstractly. He's more creative. Right?

CLAUDE
I guess so.

Jim smiles warmly at his son.

JIM
I saw the one armed man who really has two arms at the bodega.

CLAUDE
Did you give him confusing change?

JIM
I did. I tripped him up with some nickels. And a Canadian quarter.

MALCOLM
You know what I tried the other day? Sitting down to pee. Have you done this, Jim?

JIM
No...no.

MALCOLM
I did it as a lark. As a joke really. I was going to call Pauline in and say, guess what I'm doing here...

PAULINE
I'm sorry I didn't get to have that experience.

MALCOLM
I was thinking, you know, my dad used to say, "Why stand when you can sit." And this is a really good example of that. I mean, it took me so long to try because I was embarrassed.
    (to the sisters)
You guys do it all the time.

MARGOT
I never sit down in a public place. I squat and hover.

Ingrid goes wide eyed for a moment.

MALCOLM
Anyway, I recommend it. At least to try it.

PAULINE
Jim, I'm sorry about the room. It's usually Malcolm's storage room so it's kind of make-shift right now.

JIM
It's fine.

Margot stares at Jim.

JIM
Margot, open your gift.

An unopened present in blue tissue paper sits beside Margot's plate.

MARGOT
I get self-conscious opening presents in front of people. This weekend is about Pauline.

PAULINE
Oh...poo. Open it Margot.

Margot slowly unties the white ribbon and peels away the tape. Pauline groans:

PAULINE
Come on, get to it.

Margot takes out a pair of furry slippers.

MALCOLM
Those look warm.

JIM
I remember last year in Vermont you said your feet were freezing.

Her eyes find Claude who watches his parents carefully. She leans across the table to Jim and they kiss chastely and briskly on the lips.

MARGOT
Thank you.

49 INT. JIM'S CAR - NIGHT   49

Jim drives with Margot in the passenger seat.

                    MARGOT
          I already have slippers.

                    JIM
          Well, that's okay. Two sets are
          fine, right?

                    MARGOT
          It makes me sad to get a present
          that I already have.

                    JIM
          Why?

                    MARGOT
          It makes me feel like you don't
          know me.

She jams her pinky into her ear trying to get at the bug.

                    JIM
          What's wrong with your ear?

                    MARGOT
          I asked you not to come. I was so
          clear and you did it anyway so
          blithely.

                    JIM
          We need time alone to sort this
          out. You can't just run away --

                    MARGOT
          Okay, so we're here. I'm giving
          you this time.

                    JIM
               (trying a joke)
          Well, now you're putting too much
          pressure on me.

Jim smiles crookedly at her. She half-smiles back. He takes a moment, preparing to speak. Then:

                    JIM
          What is that?

His headlights catch a woman cowering at the roadside. They pass.

                        MARGOT
              Keep driving.

Jim slowly pulls over to the shoulder.

                        MARGOT
              No...no...no. Jim, no.

                        JIM
              Let me just...

Jim gets out of the car. A sobbing woman crouches, cradling a bloody dog.

                        WOMAN
              Please help me.

Jim comes toward her.

                        WOMAN
              Please help me. He got hit by a
              car. Please help me.

Margot opens her door and steps out.

                        MARGOT
                  (warily)
              Jim...

Jim kneels down by the whining pit bull. The woman screams:

                        WOMAN
              Help me!

                        MARGOT
              Careful, he might bite you!

Jim suddenly lifts up the twitching animal.

50   INT. RENTAL CAR - NIGHT   50

Jim drives, his front covered in blood. Margot is shot-gun. The lady rides in back with the panting pit in her lap.

                        WOMAN
              Hurry...he's dying. He's dying.

Margot puts her hands over her ears. Jim speeds up.

                        WOMAN
              He didn't do anything. Roger is an
              innocent. He's an innocent
              creature.

                    MARGOT
          Oh, God.

                    JIM
          Margot.

                    MARGOT
               (whispering)
          I can't stand her.

51   EXT. VETERINARY HOSPITAL - NIGHT   51

     Jim comes outside tucking his wallet in his back pocket.
     Margot sits on the car hood smoking a joint.

                    MARGOT
          You paid, didn't you?

                    JIM
          She didn't have her purse with her.
          It wasn't so expensive. Roger's
          going to live.

                    MARGOT
          I don't give a fuck about Roger.
          And...that makes me feel like shit.
          You make me feel like shit. I
          wouldn't have stopped.

                    JIM
          Of course you would've.

                    MARGOT
          No, I wouldn't've. I would have
          kept driving. I hate myself when
          I'm with you.

                    JIM
               (frustrated)
          Margot, I'm not... I can't talk to
          you when you're this fucked up.

                    MARGOT
          You're just like Claude in that
          way...you make me feel guilty.
          Sometimes I find you so despicable.

     Margot stubs out the joint on the car roof. Jim suddenly
     removes his sweater and puts it around her shoulders. He
     fishes into his pants pocket for his keys. Tears start down
     Margot's cheeks.

JIM
What's wrong?

MARGOT
I don't know.
(pause)
Before you gave me your sweater I
think I didn't realize I was cold.

Margot leans in to him, her forehead presses against his
cheek. After a moment, he puts his arms around her.

MARGOT
(quietly)
Take me home and go away.

52 INT./EXT. DINING ROOM - NIGHT   52

Margot smokes by the open door. She drinks a glass of white
wine. Pauline eats from a left-over Chinese container.

MARGOT
If it were someone else I'd
understand it, I'd feel sympathy
even. But since it's me, I just
feel bad. And horribly critical.
I haven't been able to tell Claude
what's happening. And I have to.
I'm going to.
(frustrated)
How can I be all these people? How
can I be married to Jim. And fuck
Dick. And want them both and then
neither of them...

PAULINE
I know. We're at the age where
we're becoming invisible to men and
if a guy wants to fuck us, it's
very tempting.

MARGOT
What are you saying?

PAULINE
I'm saying, if you get your sense
of self from being fuckable and
that starts to wane -- it's very
hard. I almost had an affair too.
But you know, you don't have to do
it. You can, I don't know, get a
manicure or something.

Margot grows furious. She turns to hide her face.

                    PAULINE
          You know I tell people you're my
          closest friend. I really miss you.

                    MARGOT
               (barely)
          Me too.

                    PAULINE
          But I can't help feeling that you
          really came to my wedding because I
          live a mile away from the guy
          you're fucking.

                    MARGOT
          Come on, Pauline. You make it
          sound like I'm using you.

                    PAULINE
          Yeah.

There is a long silence between them. Finally, Pauline indicates to Margot that she has something in her nostril.

                    PAULINE
          You have a...

Margot clears her nose quickly with her finger.

                    MARGOT
          Did I get it?

                    PAULINE
          Yeah, I think so.

                    MARGOT
               (suddenly)
          Paul, what are you doing getting
          married to this guy? He's not good
          enough for you. He's so coarse,
          he's like guys we rejected when we
          were sixteen. You know...don't
          make a mistake like this.
               (pause)
          I'm sorry, maybe I have no right to
          say that, but you know I'm truthful
          so... Would you rather I lie?

                    PAULINE
          Who should I be with then?

A smashing sound. Margot steps outside: Two hooded figures turn over a recycling can, glass smashes on the ground. Garbage is strewn across the driveway.

                  MARGOT (O.S.)
      Hey! Hey, you! You pick that up.
      I will call the police. This is
      our property. Pick that up.

Pauline remains seated at the table, stunned. Margot comes back inside.

                  MARGOT
      Creeps.

53   EXT. DRIVEWAY - MORNING   53

Malcolm crams the trash back in the cans. He sees something amidst the milk cartons and corn husks. He reaches down and lifts up a severed pig's hoof.

54   EXT. FIELD - MORNING   54

Claude and Ingrid idle in the tall grass calling to Wizard.

                  CLAUDE
      Dogs usually come back, I think.

                  INGRID
      What happened to your dad?

                  CLAUDE
      He went to Vermont.

                  INGRID
      He didn't want to come to the
      wedding?

                  CLAUDE
      I don't think he could... I think
      he couldn't.
        (pause)
      You want to see me dance?

                  INGRID
      Okay.

Claude dances. The gangly weeds blow around him. There's a rustling in the brush. A patch of fur catches Ingrid's eye.

                  INGRID
        (under her breath)
      Wizard...

The animal is gone.

A figure appears in the distance behind Claude. The boy, the Vogler's son, approaches shirtless in swimming trunks. Ingrid's attention goes to him.

                    CLAUDE
          You're not watching.

The boy comes into focus. He holds a dead squirrel by its tail. Ingrid backs up next to Claude. The boy stops a few feet away and hurls the squirrel at them. The kids jump back as it lands at their feet.

                    BOY
          Where are you going?

                    CLAUDE
              (stopping)
          We have to get home.

                    BOY
          Is that your girlfriend?

                    CLAUDE
          No, she's my cousin.

                    BOY
          You a fruity?

                    CLAUDE
          Um...no.

                    BOY
              (to Ingrid)
          You a fruity?

                    INGRID
              (with certainty)
          No.

                    BOY
          We will hurt you.

Claude takes Ingrid's arm and they start to walk away.

                    INGRID
          He's a Vogler.

                    CLAUDE
          He's just a stupid boy.

Claude sneaks a look over his shoulder -- the boy follows. Claude's gait quickens.

                    INGRID
          Hold it, I have a rock in my
          sandal.

                    CLAUDE
          Come on, Ingrid.

Ingrid slows, lifts her leg and removes a sandal. The boy is behind them. Claude yanks Ingrid's arm and she topples over.

                    INGRID
          Oww!

Claude leans down to help her. The boy leaps on Claude. They both crash to the ground and roll through the grass.

                    CLAUDE
          Get him off me. Ingrid!

Ingrid hesitates then runs toward the house.

Claude wrestles with the boy. The boy growls. He grabs hold of Claude's arms and sinks his teeth into Claude's shoulder.

                    CLAUDE
          Ayy! Help me!

Claude kicks and yanks himself free. He runs wildly.

Close on Claude. Tears stream down. He coughs and spits.

55   INT. HOUSE - SAME   55

Claude bursts through the front door. Ingrid sees Claude and runs to the kitchen. Margot, in a suit, goes over notes.

                    MARGOT
          Woa, don't run so fast.

                    CLAUDE
          There's a boy! He bit me!

                    MARGOT
              (alarmed)
          Who bit you?

                    CLAUDE
          A boy. A Vogler! Where's Ingrid?

                    MARGOT
          Let me see.

He tilts his head, she leans down and looks at his neck.
There are red and purple bite marks.

                    MARGOT
               (rising)
          I'm calling the police.

Claude grabs her arm.

                    CLAUDE
          No, don't! It'll get worse. Why
          did you say anything to them?

                    MARGOT
          Claude, this isn't my fault.

                    CLAUDE
          That boy bit me because you
          couldn't keep your fat mouth shut.

                    MARGOT
          Claude, you're being a jerk.

                    CLAUDE
          You shit in your shoes and then you
          fuck them!

Margot smacks Claude in the face. Ingrid stares wide eyed.

56   INT. BOOKSTORE - DAY   56

A placard reads: A Conversation with Margot Zeller and Dick
Koosman. People mull about with drinks. Pauline and Claude
admire the display of Margot's books.

                    PAULINE
          You really want to know? I'll tell
          you. She wrote a story about Lenny
          and me.
               (flips through pages)
          Yeah, it's in here. I mean we were
          talking almost every day at this
          point and there was no warning.
          Maybe a couple of remarks that
          she'd used some things of ours...
          Then The New Yorker comes -- we
          have a subscription -- and there's
          the story and... It's things we
          said and did -- stuff I told her in
          confidence.
                    (MORE)

PAULINE (CONT'D)
I think it helped end our marriage.
I read it and thought, "She hates
me."

CLAUDE
She doesn't hate you.

Pauline stares at a blown up author photo of her sister.

PAULINE
You think? Margot tried to murder
me when we were girls. She put me
on a baking sheet, sprinkled me
with paprika and put me in the
oven.

CUT TO:

The crowd files in. Margot and Dick stand in a corner.

MARGOT
Jim was here.

Dick flips through some notes.

DICK
Is Jim still writing?

MARGOT
(nods)
I told him to go to Vermont without
me.

DICK
I'd love to see him tell a linear
story for a change. Jim never
wanted to make it easy for the
reader, did he. The nicest man
I've ever met, but he can't play
the game.

MARGOT
I'm not joining him. I'm going to
stay here and then...we'll see.
Right. Okay?

DICK
I didn't ask you to do that.
(pause)
The guy's pointing at us...

58   CUT TO: 58

   Margot and Dick sit on stools holding microphones in front of
   rows of fold-out chairs. Only a few empty seats remain.
   Pauline and Claude sit in the back.

                       DICK
             I'm very interested in your story
             "Middle Children."

   Some people applaud, but it trickles off before it gets
   started.

                       DICK
             The father is a loathsome character
             yet we also feel a strange sympathy
             for him.

                       MARGOT
             Yeah, well I was very interested in
             exploring a father-daughter
             relationship. While he clings
             desperately to her, suffocates her
             really, he also silently resents
             the responsibility of parenthood.

                       DICK
             There's this sexualized push-pull
             with Daphne which I find --

                       MARGOT
             He craves isolation really. I
             always thought of him as someone
             who so over identifies with
             everyone around him that he begins
             to lose all sense of himself.

                       DICK
             You make his only recourse to
             abandon his family, including his
             beloved daughter.

                       MARGOT
             Right, that's true. That's true.

                       DICK
             I write historical fiction so I
             don't have to answer to this, but I
             wonder for someone who writes so
             nakedly about family, how
             autobiographical is this portrait?

   Margot rests her lips on the tip of the microphone.

                    MARGOT
          My father was a loving person. He
          had his days, of course, but...he
          was devoted to us as children. I
          wouldn't have written this portrait
          were it true.

Pauline nods slightly.

                    DICK
          But I'm interested in how the
          father could be in fact a portrait
          of you.

Margot stares, dumbstruck.

                    MARGOT
          Umm...I don't... Why do you assume
          it's based on... We all take from
          life. I had to have our
          refrigerator repaired the other day
          at our apartment in Manhattan. I
          was alone with a guy, I think he
          was Puerto Rican, sent over
          by...Whirlpool, I think it is who
          made our fridge. Although he said
          he worked for an independent
          organization who Whirlpool
          subcontracts. I think he was
          retarded. There was an anger in
          him and suddenly I became afraid
          for my life. I called Jim at NYU.
          I asked him to come home.

Margot stops. Her face is awash in sweat.

Pauline takes Claude's hand and presses it to her chest. His
eyes widen, fixed on his mother.

                    MARGOT
          It might be Frigidaire... I'm
          sorry... I don't... I'm not sure
          what I'm... I think I need to take
          a moment...

She stands and walks off the stage. She realizes she still
has the mike. She goes back and places it on her seat.

                    MARGOT
              (almost incoherently)
          You're an asshole...

59   INT. BOOKSTORE BATHROOM - MOMENTS LATER   59

Margot grabs a pill from her pocket, puts it on her tongue and drinks from the faucet. There is a knocking. Margot opens the door. Claude looks up at her. Pauline and Dick wait in the background.

> MARGOT
> I need to be alone right now, okay?

> CLAUDE
> What's wrong?

> MARGOT
> I don't know. I'll tell you sometime. Go on.

> CLAUDE
> Are you sure?

> MARGOT
> Yes. Go with mom. I'll see you later.

> CLAUDE
> You said, mom.

> MARGOT
> (snapping)
> But you know what I mean. Go with Pauline. Jesus, do I...do I need to spell it out for you?
> (she points)
> Go. With. Her.

60   INT. CHURCH - DAY   60

A simple, spare space, empty except for Pauline and Claude.

> PAULINE
> Are you okay?

> CLAUDE
> I'm okay.

> PAULINE
> You're your mom's favorite. Do you know that?

> CLAUDE
> I don't think she has a favorite.

PAULINE
She's always liked you best. More
than Jim even.

CLAUDE
But they're married. It's
different.

PAULINE
But she still loves you best. It's
hard, I think, to find people in
the world you love more than your
family.

CLAUDE
I like Malcolm.

PAULINE
Yeah? Good. I don't know. I do
too.
    (pause)
I can teach you to swim if you
like.

CLAUDE
No, thanks.

Claude looks at the floor. His sneaker rests next to her
open toed sandals. She taps his foot with hers.

PAULINE
Has your mother talked to you yet?

CLAUDE
I don't think so. About what?

PAULINE
Are you okay? It's hard to see
your mom like that -- get attacked
like that. Right? It was mean
what he did. I think it was really
shitty.

CLAUDE
Mm hm.

PAULINE
You know, I think your mom's going
through a rough time right now
and...whatever she tells you...like
if she says she's leaving your
father...remember that she often
changes her mind and...
    (MORE)

                    PAULINE (CONT'D)
          I don't want you to worry about
          anything right now.

Claude says nothing.

61   EXT. HOUSE - LATE DAY   61

        Pauline's Volvo rolls into the drive. She and Claude get out
        of the front seats. Margot climbs out of the back holding a
        big cake box. No one speaks.

        Malcolm, in a fleece vest and safety goggles, drags a
        chainsaw toward the oak tree. Ingrid runs to her mom.

                    INGRID
          He's cutting it down.

                    PAULINE
          Good.

        Pauline passes Maisy reading on the patio.

                    MAISY
          My dad's late to pick me up. I
          hope I'm not a pain.

                    PAULINE
          You're not a pain.

        Margot sits on the back stairs drinking a glass of wine with
        ice. The tent is up. The tables and chairs are placed
        around the lawn. She watches Malcolm prepare to take the
        tree down. She puts her pinky in her ear and twists. Claude
        approaches.

                    MARGOT
          I told Paul I didn't want you guys
          to come.

                    CLAUDE
          I thought it was interesting.

                    MARGOT
          What did Paul say?

                    CLAUDE
          I think she liked it.

                    MARGOT
          Yeah, right. Did you talk about me
          afterwards?

                    CLAUDE
          No.

MARGOT
I can tell you're lying.

CLAUDE
We didn't, mom.

MARGOT
I don't trust her.

CLAUDE
She really loves you. She does.

Margot tosses the remainder of her drink into the weeds.

MARGOT
Pauline told me she's very disappointed in you.

CLAUDE
Why?

MARGOT
She thinks you laze about the house. Ingrid is always offering to help clean or cook. She made bracelets for all the guests. Even Malcolm puts up the tent. You just wait until everyone else does it for you.

CLAUDE
That's not true.

MARGOT
It is true. You're never helpful. I wish I had taught you better manners.

CLAUDE
I can try to make popovers. If I can remember how.

MARGOT
Don't bother.

She looks at him with grave disappointment.

CLAUDE
Why are you looking at me like that?

                    MARGOT
          I just see how much you've changed.
          Your body language. You used to be
          rounder and more graceful. You're
          so stiff now. So blase.

                    CLAUDE
          What do you mean?

                    MARGOT
               (retreating)
          I can't explain it.

Margot shakes her head. She's suddenly distraught.

                    MARGOT
          It's okay though.

                    CLAUDE
          Uh huh.

Claude looks devastated. He starts toward the beach.
Margot's eyes well up -- she says, trying to make things
better:

                    MARGOT
          You're still handsome.

62   EXT. HOUSE - SAME   62

Pauline marches toward Malcolm. Malcolm wears the safety
goggles and revs the chainsaw.

                    PAULINE
          Are you able to do this yourself?

                    MALCOLM
          Pauline, do you want me to cut it
          down or not?

                    PAULINE
          Watch the tent.

The jagged blades pierce the trunk. Pauline crunches her
face. Malcolm stops suddenly.

He walks around the tree and inspects the bark.

                    MALCOLM
               (indicating his fleece)
          I liked how it looked on Vogler.

Pauline starts to say something -- stops. Then:

PAULINE
I think it's over between Dick and
Margot. He was so cruel to her
today. And poor Claude had to
watch it all. She should just get
out of the marriage and then she
can fuck whoever she wants, you
know. It's cowardly. And Dick
Koosman. What a choice. I
mean...you know?

MALCOLM
I agree. I hate the idea of Dick
fucking Margot.

PAULINE
What does that mean? You want to
fuck Margot?

MALCOLM
Pauline, that's not what I said.

PAULINE
I know you have a crush on her, you
already told me that.

Malcolm reddens and starts the chainsaw again. They yell
over the noise:

MALCOLM
I didn't say that. I said I
thought she was attractive after
you grilled me. She has no
interest in me anyway. Not that it
would matter if she did.

PAULINE
Have you ever done anything like
that.

MALCOLM
What do you mean?

PAULINE
Have you ever cheated on me?

MALCOLM
No!

Malcolm shuts the motor.

MALCOLM
Can I do this?

                    PAULINE
          Those emails you had with that
          student of mine.

                    MALCOLM
               (exhales)
          Uh huh.

                    PAULINE
          Did that...I know you said it was
          nothing.

                    MALCOLM
          It was.

                    PAULINE
          I just... Can you say it again?

                    MALCOLM
          I just did. Now, can I cut down
          the tree?

                    PAULINE
          You never did anything with her?

                    MALCOLM
          No. She emailed me after we met at
          that reading at the college and...
          You know we were friends.

                    PAULINE
          Right, just a regular friendship
          between you and a twenty year old
          girl.

                    MALCOLM
          Pauline, how many times do I have
          to say it.

                    PAULINE
          But...why don't I believe it?

                    MALCOLM
          Because Margot can't understand why
          you're with me and now when she's
          around you look for things.

                    PAULINE
               (hesitates)
          You promise.

                    MALCOLM
          I promise.

STILLS

All photos by Ken Regan

Pauline looks at him long and hard. Malcolm takes off his goggles.

                    PAULINE
          Okay. I'm sorry.

                    MALCOLM
          It's okay.

Malcolm and Pauline continue to stare at one another. He guns the chainsaw. Tears spill suddenly from his eyes. Pauline startles. He flicks the switch off.

                    MALCOLM
          I'm going to tell you something.

                    PAULINE
              (suddenly terrified)
          What?

                    MALCOLM
          I don't want to lose you, though.
          Okay?

Pauline's face goes pale.

                    MALCOLM
          I'm going to tell you... Just let
          me... Maisy...

Pauline teeters.

                    PAULINE
          I don't want to know.

                    MALCOLM
          ...we didn't really do anything.
          We were goofing around, I was
          making fun of her cause she dates a
          jock...

                    PAULINE
          I don't want to know.

                    MALCOLM
          I shouldn't've put myself in that
          position, I know that. We brushed
          lips really. It was barely a kiss.
          And then we stopped. That was it.

His nose runs. He wipes it messily with his arm.

                    MALCOLM
          Our tongues touched. I don't want
          to under-sell it either. I mean...
          We made out. I made out with her.
          I don't know why. I don't even
          like her. It's been a heady time.
                (Pauline says nothing)
          What are you thinking? Please,
          tell me what you're thinking.

     Pauline rushes at the tree -- she smacks her hands on the
     trunk and throws all her weight behind one great shove. It
     doesn't budge. In frustration and rage, she runs.

63   CUT TO: 63

     Ingrid is the only one on the patio as Pauline approaches.

                    INGRID
          Has anyone seen Wizard?

                    PAULINE
          No. Where's Maisy?

                    INGRID
          Upstairs, I think with Claude.

64   INT. PAULINE'S BEDROOM/HALLWAY - DAY   64

     Pauline enters in a daze. A toilet flushes. Maisy comes out
     of Pauline's bathroom.

                    MAISY
          Oh, hi. Sorry, I had to go. I
          hope that's okay I used yours.

     Pauline nods strangely. She goes to the window. Her dove
     grey wedding dress hangs on the back of the door.

                    MAISY
          I love your wedding dress. It's so
          unconventional and great.

     Pauline nods. Her eye catches the Polaroids of her and
     Malcolm nude which lie on top of the bureau. Maisy looks at
     the pictures too.

     Maisy shifts uneasily and leaves the room. Pauline follows.
     Maisy walks down the hallway, aware that Pauline is right
     behind her.

                    MAISY
          Is everything okay?

                    PAULINE
                (pause)
            Nothing.

Maisy stops at the landing. Claude sits at the bottom of the
staircase playing with a string.

                    MAISY
            Claude, do you want to play
            croquet?

                    CLAUDE
            Okay.

Pauline raises her leg -- her foot hovers at Maisy's lower
back. She hesitates. Claude reacts with horror. Maisy
turns around to see Pauline with her foot in the air like
she's doing karate. Pauline's eyes dart around aimlessly.

Maisy stares, confused. Pauline slowly lowers her leg.
Something dawns on Maisy. She races down the stairs.

65   EXT. HOUSE - DAY   65

The deafening shriek of the blade as it cuts into the tree.
Malcolm is soaked in sweat. Ingrid watches from a few feet
away.

In the distance -- Dick's orange BMW grinds into the
driveway. Maisy hurries toward him.

Ingrid says, buried in the noise:

                    INGRID
            There's Dick.

Malcolm sees Dick. He pushes the blade harder into the wood.

                    INGRID
            Is it almost ready?

                    MALCOLM
                (distracted)
            Almost.

Maisy is talking to her father. Dick spots Malcolm. He
immediately starts toward him. Malcolm hesitates. Cold fear
creeps up his neck.

Dick speeds up.

Malcolm backs up slowly -- drops the chainsaw -- and bolts
toward the water. Ingrid watches, confused.

Dick takes off after him. Malcolm stumbles down the long wooden stairs to the beach.

Malcolm runs wobbily -- he pants, already out of breath. Sweat pours down his face and body.

Dick's gait is swift -- his arms stiff, bent at the elbow. His jeans make a swish swish. He takes the stairs two at a time.

Malcolm grasps the railing, moving as fast as he can sideways, trying not to fall. He reaches the beach, his feet sinking in the sand. He trips and topples forward.

He looks up -- Dick lunges.

Dick pounds Malcolm's head and face. Malcolm throws his arms up and tries to block the punches.

> MALCOLM
> I didn't do anything! I didn't do anything!

> DICK
> Fucking sleazebag!

Dick gets up. He kicks Malcolm hard.

> DICK
> I don't ever want to see you again.

Malcolm balls himself up against a rock. He cries:

> MALCOLM
> Fuck off, dickhead.

Dick marches forward and kicks Malcolm again hard.

> MALCOLM
> Ow!

Dick lights a brown cigarette and walks away. Malcolm screams:

> MALCOLM
> Fucking dickbag! She's lying!

He touches his face and sees the blood on his fingers.

> MALCOLM
> (choking on tears)
> Oh, man.

There's a rustling noise in the wind. Malcolm looks -- a mud- and sea-coated Wizard watches him with a panting smile.

66 CUT TO: 66

Wheels sputter in the gravel. Dick's car peels out with Maisy in the passenger seat. Claude and Margot watch from the porch.

67 INT. LIVING ROOM/DINING ROOM - SAME   67

Pauline is seated at the table with place cards, flowers, silverware, napkins, dishes. Margot enters. Claude follows.

                    MARGOT
Come with me to New York.

                    PAULINE
I can't talk about it --

                    MARGOT
Okay, but you can't marry him. You have to go now. We can think about what to do with the baby --

                    PAULINE
        (stands)
Margot, I can't --

                    MARGOT
Don't turn vague, listen to me --

                    PAULINE
I want you to pack all your things and get out of here. You can take our car and leave it at the ferry.

                    MARGOT
        (startled)
What?

                    CLAUDE
I'll help out more. I can make popovers.

Pauline looks at Claude strangely. She leans down and kisses him on the lips.

                    PAULINE
Do you love me?
        (Claude nods)
Good.

MARGOT
Don't take this out on me? I'm on your side.

PAULINE
No, you're not. You're not.

MARGOT
I've kept my mouth shut because --

PAULINE
No, you haven't kept your mouth shut! No you haven't...kept your mouth shut...

MARGOT
Okay, I told you and I was right. He's done an insane thing. You don't know this man. What he did is criminal.

PAULINE
Margot, I can't...

MARGOT
It's pedophilia.

PAULINE
Get out!

Pauline shoves a stack of plates and silverware off of the table. The plates shatter. Silence save for their breathing.

PAULINE
Becky and I talk about you -- about what a monster you are. Is it cause Mom gave me the house? Can't I have anything? What was I thinking? I let you in. Get! Out!

MARGOT
What? What are you saying? I don't recognize you -- it's like you're channelling someone.

PAULINE
(suddenly)
Ingrid!

68   EXT. FIELD - CONTINUOUS   68

The purple of Ingrid's batik shirt shines in the grass beneath the tree.

The trunk -- a gash at its base -- teeters.

Pauline takes off into the field.

Ingrid sings to herself and traces the branches in the air with her finger.

Pauline sprints --

                         PAULINE
               Ingrid!

Ingrid says to no one in particular:

                         INGRID
               What?

Pauline's breaths are rapid, jagged.

Ingrid stands.

A wind whips up. The tree sways.

Pauline thrusts her arms out, seizes Ingrid and hurls herself away from the tree.

                         INGRID
               Ow!

Ingrid sobs as they run. Pauline looks back. The tree is still standing. They embrace a few feet out of its range.

                         INGRID
               It wasn't going to fall!

                         PAULINE
               I'm sorry.

Malcolm trudges up the stairs. He's bloody and tattered. Wizard trots behind him.

                         INGRID
               Wizard!

She hugs the dog and holds him by the collar. The three of them stand a few feet apart.

There's a horrible creak -- and suddenly --

-- crack --

Malcolm pulls both girls toward him --

The tree topples -- the thick trunk rips through the wedding tent and crashes through tables and chairs and the fence --

-- onto the Vogler's property.

69   INT. VOLVO - DAY   69

The speedometer needle wavers around 30. Margot clutches the steering wheel. Claude looks morose. Pauline and Ingrid sit stonily in the back seat. The Volvo jerks into the oncoming lane and back. Margot draws a deep breath.

                   CLAUDE
     I thought you couldn't drive.

                   MARGOT
       (irritated)
     I can drive. Why does everyone say
     that? I used to drive.

They inch up a small hill. A car cascades down past them. The Volvo shakes. Pauline suddenly snaps out of her daze:

                   PAULINE
     We have to call people and cancel.

                   INGRID
     What happened? Can I still sing?

Margot rolls down the window.

                   MARGOT
       (to Claude)
     You do smell.

                   CLAUDE
     Well, I'm not wearing any
     deodorant.

They reach the top of the hill, over the crest, and descend. The vehicle picks up speed. Margot presses down on the brake.

                   MARGOT
     Shit.

                   CLAUDE
     What?

                    MARGOT
          I don't think...
               (she pumps again)
          No... We don't have brakes.

                    PAULINE
               (resigned)
          The brakes are bad, that's right.

                    CLAUDE
          What does that mean?

                    MARGOT
          What do you think it means?

                    CLAUDE
          I mean, what can we do?

The car coasts faster down the hill.

                    CLAUDE
          Mom.

Margot places her arm stiffly across Claude's front.

Pauline wraps her body around her daughter.

Margot swerves into the shoulder -- she makes a sharp turn into the forest and crashes through the bramble and muck. The car slows until it comes to a sudden stop at the base of a tree.

70   CUT TO: 70

Margot and Claude, Pauline and Ingrid trudge through the bony white trees of the forest -- their bags weigh them down. They're all covered in sweat and there's dirt caked on their feet and ankles.

                    MARGOT
          I ruined these shoes.

Pauline's face screws up. She's suddenly in pain. She races behind a tree. Margot follows.

                    INGRID
          Mom, are you okay?

                    PAULINE (O.S.)
          Don't look!

Margot stops.

                    PAULINE (O.S.)
          Shit!

                    INGRID
          Mom, what happened?

                    PAULINE (O.S.)
          Nothing.

Margot steps to see around the trunk. The kids follow
behind. Pauline removes her panties from under her skirt.
She tosses them in the brush.

                    PAULINE
          Fuck.

Margot turns to the kids. Ingrid hides a smile.

                    CLAUDE
          Did she poop in her pants?

                    MARGOT
          It happens to everyone. Not just
          babies. It'll happen to you too
          someday.

71   EXT. FERRY - DAY   71

Margot and Claude sit, streaked with mud and perspiration.
Margot drinks a beer, Claude a Coke. Margot pops a blue pill
in her mouth and swallows. Ingrid swings on the rail.

Pauline hangs up a cell phone and hands it back to her
sister. She takes the beer and swigs.

                    PAULINE
          I left mom and Becky a message.

                    MARGOT
          I don't think mom knows how to work
          the machine.

Margot puts her pinky in her ear.

                    MARGOT
          I can hear it flapping.

                    PAULINE
          You should take care of that. It
          can hatch eggs.

Claude turns his head. In the Chevy next to them sits Mrs. Vogler and the Vogler boy. She sings along to the radio. She runs her hand through her son's hair gently. He nestles into her shoulder.

72 EXT. SEASIDE TOWN STREET - EVENING   72

The four of them get out of a taxi. A small, peeling hotel.

73 INT. HOTEL ROOM - CONTINUOUS   73

A dark tight space with a faded and dirty green wall-to-wall carpet. Pauline combs Ingrid's hair on one of the two double beds. Ingrid practices her wedding song. Claude sits on the other bed and looks into the open bathroom door: Margot stands with her back to him. She talks on her cell phone in a whisper. She hangs up. Claude walks inside. The sink drips.

                    MARGOT
          Sweety, there's a bus that leaves
          to Vermont from town tomorrow
          morning. I just talked to your dad
          and he's going to pick you up.

                    CLAUDE
          Aren't you coming?

                    MARGOT
          No.

                    CLAUDE
          Why not?

                    MARGOT
          I have to help out Paul and Ingrid.

Claude tugs gently on his yellow bracelet.

                    CLAUDE
          I don't want to go tomorrow.

The distant bong of a low drum and beneath that -- chanting. Claude follows Margot to the window. Ingrid and Pauline are already looking out.

Clumps of demonstrators march in the street. Some people hold up signs with slogans -- NO MORE -- BRING BACK -- the rest is obscured from the window. Some marchers are dressed in black hoods with white face paint and carry cardboard coffins.

PAULINE
There's Malcolm.

Pauline points to a guy in a vest. As he turns around we see it isn't him. Pauline withdraws, suddenly on the verge of tears.

PAULINE
I can't live in that house alone.

MARGOT
You're going to be fine.

PAULINE
Maybe...maybe I could get a place in Brooklyn -- Williamsburg or something. People are living there right?

MARGOT
You don't want to live there. It's all young people.

PAULINE
But what do you think of that idea?

MARGOT
Maybe. Let's see. You know if you don't want to come with me, I'm sure mom will let you stay with her --

PAULINE
(through tears)
You're already trying to pass me off on mom...

MARGOT
Don't say that. Come on, you'll come home with us.

PAULINE
You don't even know where you're going to live. You might have to move in with mom too.

Margot tightens.

PAULINE
What? Oh.
(mouthing a whisper)
Didn't you tell him?

Margot looks at her son who continues to watch out the window.

74 CUT TO: 74

Pauline emerges from behind the armoire doors wearing a long nightshirt that reads: I Spent The Night With Arsenio Hall. She enters the bathroom. She mutters to herself.

                    PAULINE
          What have I done? What have I
          done?

Margot jimmies up the stiff window to let in some air. A few stragglers still march in the street. Trash and pieces of signage line the gutter. Margot turns into the room. She puts her hand to her cheek and strokes her smooth skin. She watches her son who removes his jeans for bed.

                    CLAUDE
          What?

                    MARGOT
          Nothing. Just then I felt so much
          love for you.

75 CUT TO: 75

Pauline tucks in Ingrid who lies next to Claude. Margot sits on the other bed scribbling in her brown notebook. Pauline marches around and across to the other side of the room. She snatches the book out of Margot's hands.

                    MARGOT
          Hey!

                    PAULINE
          You cannot write about this. You
          can't have it.

                    MARGOT
          I wasn't writing about you.

                    PAULINE
          You already took a part of my life,
          you can't have any more. And that
          goes for Ingrid and Malcolm and
          Wizard. We all own our own rights.
          They're not for sale.

                    MARGOT
          Give it back.

Pauline glances at the book.

                    PAULINE
          If I could read your handwriting
          I'm sure I'd be furious. But if I
          ever see a story that involves a
          hotel room or any of this shit, I
          will fucking take your bowels out.

Pauline thrusts the book back at Margot --

CUT TO:

The kids sleep in one bed. Margot and Pauline lie awake in the other.

                    PAULINE
          You've now successfully ruined two
          of my marriages.

                    MARGOT
          You're not wearing any underwear.

                    PAULINE
          It's hot, I'm pregnant. Move over.
          Jesus.

                    MARGOT
          You're not hot, your feet are cold.

                    PAULINE
          Stop touching me. I am so hot.
          Feel my head.

Margot puts her lips to Pauline's forehead.

                    MARGOT
          You have a fever.

                    PAULINE
          I don't have a fever... I'm
          pregnant...are you always like
          this?

                    MARGOT
          Get used to it... Mom and Becky
          share a bed -- you and I will
          probably get the other.

                    PAULINE
          You should just go to Vermont.

                    MARGOT
          I was thinking -- you know if you
          want -- you and Ingrid could go to
          Vermont. Keep Claude company and
          Jim adores you.

                    PAULINE
          You don't like Malcolm because
          you're not attracted to him.

                    MARGOT
          Will you do it?

                    PAULINE
          No. I won't do that for you.

                    MARGOT
               (pause)
          Did you two talk about me in town?
          What did you say?

                    PAULINE
               (pause)
          I told him you often change your
          mind.

76   INT. BAR/RESTAURANT - MORNING   76

Cheap plastic tables. A small karaoke stage in front.
Margot, Claude, Pauline and Ingrid sit at the bar. Margot
drinks her wine with ice. She wears Jim's sweater. The kids
have Cokes. The remains of ketchup-soaked french fries in a
plastic red basket lie between them.

A man with a mullet climbs up on the karaoke stage. The
music begins. The man sways and sings "On and On" by Stephen
Bishop. He croons sweetly and beautifully. Claude's eyes
moisten. Margot swallows a blue pill and chases it with the
wine. She takes her son's hand and whispers:

                    MARGOT
          I'm sorry, sweety. There's
          something wrong with me.

                    PAULINE
          I'm going to call him.

Margot quickly turns to her sister.

                    MARGOT
          No. Don't. I'm telling you.

                    PAULINE
          I...I need some clothes and things.

                    MARGOT
          He should get the hell out of <u>our</u>
          house.

                    PAULINE
          Okay. I'll tell him to get the
          hell out of our house.

Pauline walks over to a pay phone.

CUT TO:

Pauline holds the receiver to her ear. She stares at a drawing of a monster fucking a woman on the wall above the pay phone. Malcolm is crying.

                    MALCOLM'S VOICE
          The tent looks so lonely.

                    PAULINE
          It has no one to get married in it.

EXT. HOUSE - INTERCUT

Malcolm sits in the grass, the tree and wreckage behind him.

                    MALCOLM
          I know. And it's smashed. I'm
          such a fucking idiot. Please don't
          take me seriously. I mean take me
          seriously, but not the fucked up
          parts, you know. I love you so
          much. Please marry me.

                    PAULINE
          You can't do what you did again.
          Do you understand?

                    MALCOLM
          I promise.

                    PAULINE
          No matter how tempting.

At the bar: Margot watches her sister carefully. She absent-mindedly picks through her red knit bracelet and drops it onto the floor.

Ingrid slides something small and grey across the bar to Claude.

                              INGRID
                    You left it in my room.

It's a piece of fingernail. He hesitates then puts it in his
pocket.

At the phone: Pauline rests her head against the wall.
Malcolm is bawling on the other end.

                              PAULINE
                    I don't know. I don't know.

Malcolm clutches Wizard and sputters:

                              MALCOLM
                    I ate some of the cake. I don't
                    know why, but I did it.

                              PAULINE
                    What was... How was it?

                              MALCOLM
                    Good.

                              PAULINE
                    It's not too sweet? They sometimes
                    make their stuff too sweet.

                              MALCOLM
                    Maybe. Maybe it was. I didn't
                    even notice... They fucked up the
                    cake. How sad. I love our little
                    baby. I miss you.

                              PAULINE
                    I miss you too. Maybe we should do
                    another seminar.

Malcolm says something incomprehensible.

                              PAULINE
                    I can't understand you, honey.

Margot finishes her glass of wine, her eyes still on her
sister.

                              INGRID
                    There's gramma and Aunt Becky!

Margot startles and looks out the window. Across the street
is an older woman, 70's, and a large woman, mid 30's, eating
ice cream cones and looking in a boarded-up shop window.

                    PAULINE
          They didn't get my message.

Pauline now stands above them.

                    MARGOT
          I told you she can't work the
          machine --

Ingrid's chair scrapes as she stands. She takes her mother's
hand. Margot remains seated.

                    PAULINE
          What? You're not coming?

                    MARGOT
          I'm coming, I'm coming. What did
          he say?

Pauline and Ingrid head for the door. Claude waits for
Margot.

                    MARGOT
          What did he say?

She grabs her bags and drops some bills on the table.

                    MARGOT
              (to herself)
          Don't worry, I got it.

79   EXT. STREET - MORNING   79

The sisters and children come outside. The mother and Becky
now idle further down the street.

                    PAULINE/INGRID
          Mom!/Nana!

Margot takes Claude's arm and walks quickly in the opposite
direction. Claude, confused, glances over his shoulder.

                    MARGOT
          Don't look. Keep walking.

                    CLAUDE
          Why are we --

                    MARGOT
          We have to get you to your bus.

80   CUT TO: 80

A huge parking lot. A bus in the distance. Claude tries to keep pace with his mother.

                    CLAUDE
          Did you do something?

                    MARGOT
          What do you mean, do something?

                    CLAUDE
          I mean, why is the wedding not
          happening? Is there something that
          you did?

                    MARGOT
          Pauline has transferred all her
          stuff onto me. I don't understand
          her anymore. Why'd she pick this
          man? It is really berserk. And
          you know, she referred to me as her
          closest friend. We never see one
          anoth --

An unfamiliar sound comes out of Margot. The sadness is unexpected -- she sobs uncontrollably. She tries to speak:

                    MARGOT
          I mean we're not close. Even if we
          want to be. You know?

                    CLAUDE
          But was there anything real?

                    MARGOT
          No! How many times do I have to
          say it? Jesus. You think so
          little of me.
               (through her sobs)
          It's good you're going. You
          shouldn't be around me either. I'd
          go if I were you...

                    CLAUDE
          Will you find Pauline and Nana
          after I leave?

                    MARGOT
               (half-serious)
          I don't know. Maybe I'll go to
          church.

Margot is sweating. She wipes her brow with her sleeve. She periodically looks behind her. Nobody seems to be following.

                  CLAUDE
            (growing nervous)
   Are you angry at me?

                  MARGOT
   No, honey. I'm not mad at you.

                  CLAUDE
   I don't want to go with you mad at anyone.

                  MARGOT
   Everything's fine. I'm not mad at anyone.

Up ahead is a tiny depot. People climb onto a white bus.

                  CLAUDE
   Can you come with me?

                  MARGOT
   No, you know that.
      (pause)
   We should talk about the next few months a little bit and what's going to happen --

                  CLAUDE
   I don't like Vermont.

                  MARGOT
   Your dad will be very happy to see you. And I'm sure Josh is dying to hang out.

                  CLAUDE
   Please come, mom.

                  MARGOT
      (suddenly irritable)
   Claude, stop it. Okay?

She watches a man sustain a long embrace with another man. Margot closes her eyes. She breathes deeply.

                  MARGOT
   You used to need me to watch you when you played.

CLAUDE
What do you mean?

MARGOT
(vaguely)
When you first started to play with friends, you wouldn't do it unless I watched you. You were afraid I would go out the back door. I don't know where I would go. Our yard didn't lead anywhere anyway.

She takes off her sweater and reveals an old faded yellow T-shirt. She isn't wearing a bra. Claude says suddenly:

CLAUDE
I masturbated last night. While everyone was asleep I went into the bathroom and did it.

MARGOT
You don't have to tell me, sweety.

The bus driver slams the luggage compartment closed.

MARGOT
You've got to go.

Margot ties her sweater around her waist and takes Claude's hand. They approach the bus. Claude's body tenses.

CLAUDE
How will you get home?

MARGOT
I don't know. I'll see. Maybe Dick can drive me to the...
    (pause)
Jesus, I lost the word for a second. The train.

CLAUDE
Uh huh.

He looks at her longingly.

MARGOT
Come on. You always don't want to leave me and you always have a good time once you do.
    (provocatively)
I think you like getting away from me.

CLAUDE
I do not. I like hanging out with
you.

She hugs him. He clutches her.

CLAUDE
The world feels strange to me right
now.

Margot nods sympathetically. She kisses his lips and
releases him. He reaches into his bag and shyly puts on his
wrap-around punk sunglasses. Margot makes a face.

CLAUDE
What?

MARGOT
They make your face look too wide.

Claude removes them and puts them back in the bag.

CLAUDE
See you soon.

MARGOT
Bye, sweety.

CLAUDE
Say, you'll see me "soon."

MARGOT
You're acting like a baby.

She backs away --

CLAUDE
Don't see Dick.

MARGOT
Don't worry. I don't think he
wants to see me anyway.

CLAUDE
Please, Margot. Promise me.

MARGOT
(hesitates)
Don't call me that.

Claude doesn't move. Margot points at the bus and mouths
"Go". She turns in the other direction. Claude, frustrated
and anxious approaches the vehicle.

| 81 | INT. BUS - CONTINUOUS | 81 |

Claude hurries toward the back and finds a window seat. He puts his bag next to him and looks out the dirty glass.

Claude's POV: Margot, her back to him, puts her finger in her ear and shakes her head.

The sweater around her waist loosens and drifts to the pavement. She starts walking.

The bus hisses and lurches forward. Claude strains to see:

Margot looks back.

The bus groans as it picks up speed. Margot sprints.

> MARGOT
> Wait!

She's runs full speed, waving her arms wildly.

> MARGOT
> Wait! Wait!

She pants, breathless.

The bus brakes.

She passes Claude's window. We stay on Claude. He waits. Finally, she appears next to him, covered in sweat, and panting. She kisses him on the head. The bus starts moving.

> MARGOT
> (almost euphoric)
> Did you see me running out there?

> CLAUDE
> Yeah.

Margot cranes her neck to see outside.

> MARGOT
> Good. That was a lot of running.
> I'm out of breath.

Claude turns away from his mother and looks out the window.

CUT TO BLACK.

Q & A

WITH NOAH BAUMBACH
BY ROB FELD

How do you think about the opening moment of a film? **The Squid and the Whale** *opens with that tense tennis scene, and* **Margot** *begins with a close-up of Claude's hand.*

Noah Baumbach: Both *Squid* and *Margot* begin in the middle of the action. It's less about establishing a place than about creating an energy. An earlier draft of *Squid* had a scene that eased you in before the tennis scene, but I cut it for that very reason—it was too gentle. With *Margot*—after the *Squid* experience—I was very aware of how I wanted the movie to begin. It's a kid on a moving train: everything is moving. The scenery keeps changing, as does his perception—he sits next to the wrong person, then next to the right person (his mother), but for the rest of the movie his understanding of his mother is changing. Is she a stranger, too? It's a child's perspective—you're on a certain height level. I remember how embarrassing it was if you took the hand of, or sat next to, someone who wasn't your parent. But since it's the beginning of the movie, the audience doesn't know yet that it's the wrong person.

You learn it as you go. The abruptness of the opening also emphasizes that we're catching these people in the midst of their lives. They've existed before the movie, and they'll live on after the credits. It's something that's done

---

Rob Feld interviewed Noah Baumbach in Los Angeles on August 2, 2007. Feld is a writer and independent producer at Manifesto Films. His writings on film and interviews with such noted filmmakers as James L. Brooks, Charlie Kaufman, Bill Condon, Peter Hedges, Noah Baumbach, Mike Nichols, and Alexander Payne appear regularly in *Written By* magazine and *DGA Quarterly*, as well as in the Newmarket Shooting Script® series.

more explicitly in documentaries and mock documentaries, where you're aware of the camera and what they're selecting to show you. I'm interested more and more in making movies that are experiences for the audience—that don't have a lot of reaction shots, don't have markers to tell you how to feel about a scene or person. I think the opening of the movie properly sets the tone and lets you know it's not going to do the work for you.

And set the grammar, as well.

NB: Yes, that's true, too. From a filmmaking perspective, we're handheld on the back of Claude's head, walking, letting him lead us. The movie is shot-listed and organized, but the illusion of the movie is that the characters are leading us, not us leading them. And that's all there in the first shot.

Were you watching vérité *documentaries, where the camera tries to blend in with the goings-on? You started using a like sensibility in* Squid.

NB: I watched a lot of Maysles, Wiseman, and Pennebaker for *Squid* because it was the first time I shot this way. On *Margot* I knew instinctually how I wanted to shoot it. A lot of influence from other movies had seeped in along the way.

What happened between the sharp, polished comedies you made before and this time, where the aesthetic is far more rough-hewn? Changes in you, in what you were trying to do?

NB: A little of everything. It's likely that eventually I'll write something again that feels less rough and should be shot on sticks, or with Steadicam, or on a dolly. The script of *Squid* just called for a different way of shooting. And *Margot* continues this. That said, I changed after the experience of *Kicking and Screaming* and *Mr. Jealousy*. I had different ideas about how I wanted to make movies. It doesn't mean it was a conscious response to what I had already done; it was a development for me.

You've spoken about a handmade quality that method of shooting Squid *gave, which is probably even more apt with* Margot. *Does that have the effect of making it feel more human?*

NB: I think so, although I don't think consciously about the rough edges. I just allow them to happen and appear. I'm not interested in doing it as a style—and you've seen that in movies, where they rub your nose in the grit. I don't want the movies to feel grimy. I want them to be beautiful, in their way. And I find it beautiful—in *Margot* there are a lot of scenes of people in the house during the day with no lights on. Their faces go dark, but it's how your eye sees in real life. It's also a way I like working with the camera and with actors—there's a controlled freedom in the way we capture the action when we don't have to light all day. I could say the style is that there's no style, but that's not really true, either.

After I described to Harris Savides the look I wanted, he suggested these old lenses. We flashed the 35mm film and that, in concert with these lenses (we pretty much used a 35mm and a 50mm the whole time) and mostly natural light and practicals, gave us a very specific look. The best I can describe it is as some combination of old color family photographs and some diffuse quality that memory has. But it doesn't call attention to itself. We also didn't do a digital intermediate; we wanted to emphasize the film quality. Harris and I value the same things in film.

Even in* Kicking and Screaming, *I should say, the camera is always moving.

NB: With *Kicking and Screaming* we were on dollies a lot. I was thinking more of Jean Renoir camera movement. With *Margot*, it's handheld like *Squid*—held steadily. It allows the camera a flexibility, but it's about the characters, not the camera movement. At the same time you feel a human presence. It feels captured, in a way.

Margot *felt like a great deal of natural light, and it was very dark at moments. Did you do much lighting at all?*

NB: We lit a little, we had to. Light changes through the day, and we didn't have a long enough shooting schedule—forty-two days—to pull a *Days of Heaven* and just come back and shoot magic hour again the next day. Even if we started shooting with no lights, we would have to light at some point as the sun changed, so that the shots would match. Some scenes were simply practicals or natural light, and Harris and I often fantasized about shooting the same time of day over a sequence, but there was no way we'd get the movie done.

There's very little air in* Margot. *How have you come to think about getting from one scene to another?

NB: I like this idea of scenes crashing into each other. It goes along with what I was saying about it feeling like an experience, or our perception of experience. I often don't know, in my regular life, how I feel in the middle of a conversation with someone, for example. Often that comes later, after I've had time to digest it. *Margot* is structured that way, and it may be a new way for some people to watch a movie. I think an audience, understandably, wants to figure out what they feel about a character or a scene as it's happening. *Is that person being mean to this person? Does the person deserve it or are they the victim?* I got it a lot with *Squid*, and now with this, too, where people have very different, personal reactions. People identify with different characters and differ in whether they think something is funny or not. But that would be true in life, too, if these characters existed. The movies, also, aren't really about one person. They're kind of ensembles, but they don't announce themselves as ensembles—so you have to figure that out for yourself, too.

Was this way of dealing with transitions something with which you approached* Squid, *or was it something that, while working, you kind of discovered and started playing with?

NB: In many areas the script of *Squid* had more traditional scene endings than wound up in the movie. In the script for *Margot*—and now we're talking about this in a far more conscious and theoretical manner than I was thinking at the time—the scenes are often interrupted by other scenes. It approximates our memory of things. Our everyday experiences don't have establishing shots, they don't announce themselves, they're frequently obtuse and hard to decipher. Sometimes, in a movie, you need those things to convey information, and there are scenes in *Margot* that end maybe more comfortably than others, but in general I want the audience to participate. I think this can be very pleasurable.

I like when scenes turn into other scenes. For example: Margot at the table when Allan and Toby are coming to dinner. We cut in the middle of Margot's line and bang—we're into Pauline dropping the plates in the kitchen. That was in the script. Some interruptions weren't scripted. While cutting the movie I'd think, *Wouldn't it be great if we were just into the next scene?* You can still be reflecting on the piece you just saw when you're into the next one. If you think about it in that way, then it's okay for the scenes to bleed over or get interrupted. I do it with sound, too. When John and Nicole take the dog to the vet, that scene ends with them embracing and her saying, "Take me home and go away." It wasn't scripted but she gave an exhale, which I found very moving. When Carol Littleton and I were cutting the movie, we tried different ways of doing it, but the exhale actually carries over onto Jennifer's face as she's eating Chinese food in the following scene. When we cut back to Nicole, she's recovered, and talking about it intellectually—she's not as emotional. I'm working those transitions more now in the scripts, but I also think that when you're cutting and bringing in sounds and music, and actors have reinvented the roles, you want to go with those moments.

Back to the idea of ambiguity, what did you find to be the greatest challenge of making the thing readable?

NB: Mostly I can tell when it sounds right. The scripts start very intuitively—the early drafts are much more ambiguous. The harder work is shaping them and figuring out what story you're telling—what is the movie? That's really the rewriting process and getting the right people to read it—in this case, both Jennifer and Scott Rudin are great at seeing things that I don't necessarily see. Sometimes it's about clearing things up; other times it's about pushing ideas or events that are living in the margins out to the forefront.

You'd said you wanted the flashback scenes in Kicking and Screaming like Chris Marker's La Jetée. You've also said you might have the guts not to cue the audience that they were entering flashbacks in the same way, if you did it now.

NB: That's probably true, and I'd probably shoot them differently, too. At least, I'd be more conscious of what the first shot going into them would be. Those are things you learn.

Would you shoot that film differently now?

NB: Of course I'd shoot it differently now, but part of what's best about that movie is that I was twenty-five when I made it and it was about a time in life that I'd just lived through. That's something you can't quantify, change, or improve upon. Similarly, the nice thing about having kids in movies is that you're getting them at this moment in time—even while shooting, their shoe sizes are changing. And *Kicking and Screaming* is me at that time. Because I was twenty-five then and I'm thirty-seven now I would do things differently, but I don't know that I would improve upon it, either.

There's no score in Margot, but there are songs. How have you come to think about the use of music, in this film in particular?

NB: The movie is cut very tightly, but I was curious what score would feel like, so I had Britta Phillips and Dean Wareham, who did the score for *Squid and the Whale*, come in and watch a cut of the movie. We had some ideas, and they wrote some pieces that sounded really interesting. But, during this whole period, I have to admit I felt like I was doing my due diligence. I was curious, but the movie was working so well as it was. And it was very quickly apparent that no matter what you tried, even if you went against the scene, any kind of underscore didn't work. The scenes, by design, aren't telling you what they're about, so even score that was designed *not* to comment on anything had its own comment.

But it highlighted my intention—that these scenes could be read in many different ways. Some of the songs become score-like. There's a Fleetwood Mac song on the ferry, which carries over into the hotel, so it could never actually be a source cue, if you want to get literal. But there's a ton of music in the movie, and it's all stuff that the characters are playing. I haven't used a lot of score in any of my movies. *Squid* has a few montage scenes and a little underscore, and songs are used as score. In *Kicking and Screaming* I only used score going into the flashbacks. I think I was more timid in that movie. I was confident in terms of my musical taste, but less sure of how I wanted to use music. That was true of sound, too, on that movie. I feel like on each movie I learn a new trade of directing. In *Squid* I think I learned to edit. On *Margot* I learned sound in a different way.

Along with the visuals, the sound is very rough in Margot, as well. What did you not do?

NB: We didn't loop anything. We use pretty much all of the recorded sound. But we built in a lot of effects as well—layered in the atmosphere of the house and water. It's designed so that you won't notice, but I reached further with sound than I had in the past.

How about creating environments for characters to exist in: Bernard's car in Squid, *the old house in* Margot? *I can't remember really seeing an establishing shot of the house, until maybe later, but you had such a sense of the house, anyway. When do you start thinking about the details of those environments?*

NB: When I'm writing. Anne Ross—who did the production design on both movies—and I both really like thinking about what people have in their homes. With the books, we thought a lot about what people had brought there and left behind, things from their childhoods, bestsellers of summers past. The old videotapes, the records, the history of a stain on the wall. The desired effect, obviously, when it's done is that all of these things blend in. There's the aesthetic side of it, too—the textures, the colors of the walls. It's also a practical matter: *How dark can we paint the walls if we're flashing the film?* You learn all that stuff in tests. But it's most important to get the anthropology of these people right, even if it's a taste that I don't share. Some of it is written into the script, some of it I leave out just to keep the page count down, and some of it you come to later.

Do you have a favorite secret you thought was so telling but that didn't make it into the movie?

NB: On the refrigerator in the kitchen there's a number that you pin to your shirt when you're running a race—I was thinking something like the island six-kilometer race that Pauline may have run. It's peeking out, covered by magnets and photos. There's also a photo on the fridge of Flora Cross, who plays Ingrid, in a Dracula thing, that's a real childhood picture of Flora's. It's nice to bring in people's real things and make them character things. There's books and records in the movie that I could point out. We also have the scene where Margot goes through Pauline's things, and that's a way to actually show the little artifacts. That's something in the script where I was pretty specific about what the pills were, but when we were actually shooting it, none of that mattered.

Dividing it into adults and children, how have you been working with actors, how have your thoughts on that developed? What did you learn from Squid? **You cast such great, fearless kids.**

NB: I always hear the script a certain way. I have this sense of how it all sounds, though I couldn't tell you exactly and I'm not always particularly good at giving line readings. I think I know when it sounds right. But I can be wrong or they can do it better sometimes. I can think I have it and then use a different take in editing because I realize that my view may have been limited, and they actually expanded upon it and did something better. I think most of the time I can feel when lines or moments are right. I acted a bit in college and I've been around actors a lot in my life, so I feel sympathetic to them, but I don't have any training in directing and I'm always interested in hearing directors who came from the theater speak about acting. They seem so assured when they talk about a text or the motivation of a character. I'm sure they work on feel as well. I just talk to actors as I talk to anyone, in all my halting ways, cutting myself off mid-sentence and starting some other thought. I try to be as clear as I can, obviously, but sometimes I'm still figuring it out as I'm saying it. The rehearsal process allows for me to learn the actors and for them to learn me. A lot of what we do is talk about the characters or go on tangents from our own lives. Then when we're on set, we have an easier way of communicating with each other, and that was very much the case with *Margot*.

With actors like Jennifer and Nicole, they're very alive in each take. Whatever was specific about that take—a change in the wind, if somebody misses a line or knocks into something—influences them. I can see it in the scene where they're walking in the woods, which is a long take. A branch almost hits Jennifer and she moves it out of the way, Nicole loses her footing for a moment; and I see, because I've seen maybe eleven of those, how it affects the line that comes out next. That's really exciting when you have actors that do that. They're also professionals, so they know what the scene requires, but they're leaving themselves open. I think that's kind of incredible.

With kids it's this whole other thing because you don't want them to be able to do the same thing over and over again, because that's when you get lousy kid acting. You want a kid who's alive, in the moment, too, but obviously since they don't have the training that Nicole and Jennifer have, it's a riskier situation. Some takes can be me talking, talking, talking—giving direct instructions or a line reading or some complete non sequitur—them saying the line; me talking, talking, talking, them saying the line—which can be horrible to listen to in post production. But that's the trade-off because then you get these great, natural moments.

Zane, for instance, I discovered, was able to connect to the feelings of the character—he could really act. But it's scary for a kid. You don't want them too out of control because then they can't say the line. He had some really emotional scenes where I would help connect him to those feelings. I admit I have fantasies of being one of those directors—what I imagine Werner Herzog, Lars von Trier, or John Cassavetes did—who slaps an actor, then shoots the scene. Those darker thoughts go through your head when you're having trouble. But I don't do that. I think the actor would just slap me back.

How much rehearsal did you have?

NB: Two official weeks. I worked with Nicole and Jennifer in the house—we'd run scenes and hang out. We probably spent more time talking about the characters and relationships than reading the lines. With actors like that, they're so good, the scenes get good quickly, so I don't want to burn it out. You get it almost there. We all lived on location, next to one another, during the shoot, so there were a lot of dinners, game nights. Jack introduced a great game with the Leonard Maltin Movie Guide.

How do you cast?

NB: Jennifer keeps discovering the kids. She suggested Owen Kline for *Squid*, and Zane's mother (Lisa Emery) was in a play (Mike Leigh's "Abigail's Party") with Jennifer. Jennifer saw Zane doing his homework backstage and suggested him. We brought him over to the apartment—he got the more ideal audition situation—we hung out with him and had him read. Then he read with Doug Aibel, the casting director—I wanted to see how he'd do in a more pressurized situation. He hadn't acted before, but he was very assured and really understood what he was doing in a way that was kind of amazing. I was simultaneously reading lots of kids, but he kept rising to the top. Flora had been in *Bee Season*, but I hadn't seen it. She was really good really fast. I brought her in with Zane and it was an easy decision.

What films were you watching while working on Margot? I keep thinking Bergman…and the underwater swimming pool shot and ending on the bus made me think The Graduate.

NB: I hadn't thought of *The Graduate*. Actually, there is a shot with Jennifer laughing after Nicole gets stuck in the tree, and I was thinking very consciously of another Mike Nichols movie: the shot in *Carnal Knowledge* of Candice Bergen laughing. A lot of scenes in *Carnal Knowledge* are shots of just one person while you hear the others offscreen, rather than the traditional way of starting wide before going in. I didn't rewatch *Carnal Knowledge* before doing this, so I could be wrong, but it's my impression of the film.

In terms of the writing, characters, and story, I wasn't thinking of specific movies, but when I started work on *Margot* I had been watching a combination of Rohmer and 1960s-era Bergman—a lot of the stuff that takes place on his island Faro: *The Passion of Anna*, *Shame* and *Hour of the Wolf*, *Persona*. *Passion of Anna*, particularly, because that one's in color. It has a feeling of loneliness, but it has great scenes with groups at dinner that probably went into my thinking of doing something in the country, and maybe on an island. But I'd also spent a couple of summers as a kid on an island, and I was thinking of those feelings and memories of being on a ferry, and isolated from the mainland. It's always tricky when you talk about movies that influence you because they frequently spark things that an outsider wouldn't know or recognize.

Similar to music, I would think? You could be listening to things that don't actually wind up in the movie.

NB: Exactly. That happens all the time. You put together a playlist and none of those things end up in the movie. It's what gets you there, but then there's what you wind up with, and you have to acknowledge the difference. A lot of times you can feel the difference because the song just doesn't sound right. Eric Rohmer's *La Collectionneuse* was another film I watched; Néstor Almendros shot it and I don't think they used any additional lighting. Néstor wrote a great book called *Man with a Camera,* where he talks about all his movies. They had so little money that when they did a shot and then reverse, they planned ahead which lines were going to be on camera, so they wouldn't have to shoot the whole scene on both sides. The lab thought it was a short, they shot so little film. That's another great movie, and it also takes place in the country.

The Bergman movies and that movie deal a lot, too, with the psychology of the individual versus the physical world, the relationship of the inside and outside. I was more conscious in this movie of depicting the physical world versus the internal world, and that's something those two filmmakers do brilliantly. *Hour of the Wolf* is nothing like *Margot at the Wedding,* but it's about madness and how the mind distorts perception. I was thinking about that a lot in *Margot* with the neighbors—how they're perceived versus who they really are. The characters in *Margot* are all going through transitions that are scary and new: Claude is going through adolescence, Margot is leaving her husband, Pauline and Malcolm are getting married—all of these things can make you feel out of control. Some things you choose and others happen to you.

What type of scenes are you enjoying shooting or writing now?
NB: The first major scene with Pauline and Margot, where Pauline brings her sister into the bedroom—Margot is unpacking and Pauline is updating her on what's been happening. Margot walks to the closet and back to the bed, Pauline goes out into the hall to get towels and comes back in. The scene established the relationship between the sisters. Jennifer and Nicole were so good in it but it had movement, so it was more fun to shoot than, say, five people at a dinner table. We didn't do it in any sort of traditional way—we'd follow one character some of the time and then switch it up—and it got a little sloppy at times; I'd nudge the cameraman, "Go follow her now," and we'd get some weird angles.

It was funny because, even in the editing, I felt like I had way more takes of a certain angle than I actually did. We kind of modified it as we shot the movie and became more adult and professional about it all. But I loved shooting it that way, and Harris and I talked about finding a way to do it more often. There's so much crap on a movie set that has to be there but is a distraction. You want to pare it away as much as you can. The closest you can get to just turning on the camera and having the actors do the scene, that's the most fun. Shooting around a table is a chore because you have to turn around and get everybody, worry about eye-lines. I write scenes at tables, scenes with eating, because I spend a lot of my life doing it and I like observing people doing it, but it's less fun to shoot.

The women walking in the woods was also pleasurable—it was one take, the cameraman walking backwards, me walking behind him. There was a point in the shooting where, it had been a hard day with bad weather—it was one of those days in the middle of the shoot that just felt *long*. The last scene of the day was the one in the den, post-swimming, where Pauline asks Margot if she can go to Margot's bookstore conversation. I had planned to shoot coverage, but I just said, you know, I've got these two great actors, let's just shoot it all in a master. It could have backfired as just a dumb, reckless, tired move. But it's another scene I love to watch, and in the context of the movie it's nice to have everything slow down to a long, steady single take.

You'd think I'd instinctually write scenes I'd like to shoot, but it doesn't always work that way. When I'm writing, I'm thinking of the characters as real, with real lives, so they end up eating and in cars and sitting and sleeping—maybe not the most dynamic cinematic moments. Sometimes later I'll try to bring in more movement. The car stuff is particularly tough because I don't use rigs and always insist on getting in the car with the actors, which gets really uncomfortable.

Structurally, Margot *is constantly unfolding.*

NB: I think this movie maintains the discovery I had as a writer in that it propels forward without letting you know what's coming. It was heavily rewritten and restructured over many drafts, but as you're watching it I don't think you feel where it's going. This might be difficult for people who like the comfort of knowing what's coming, but I prefer this tension, which can cause anxiety and giddy pleasure sometimes simultaneously.

Many of your characters, in many of your films, are stifled by the great expectations put upon them—by others or by themselves—or are closed off to others for that reason. How do you visually approach that?

NB: A lot of that is a feeling thing. When I shot-list the movie, my first pass through it is as it comes to me. Up until that point, it's something I've both thought about a lot and not thought about at all. There's a real compartmentalization while I'm writing. I'm not thinking about actors, I'm often not thinking about shots. Obviously, at a certain point—like sleep—another semiconscious part of my brain is formulating all those things at the same time. I just don't let it affect the writing so much. I think the writing should stay in the realm of fantasy as long as it can. There's going to be a time soon enough when you say, This actor's got this color hair now and we're going to have to change that line because the car is now on his left.... But mostly, I feel like I have a pretty good sense of the feel of the scene and how close we should be, how far away, how much coverage I'm going to do. I like for people to move in and out of rooms, in and out of houses, from a lit room to a dark room, etc., and this way we can easily walk with them. This method also allows us to adjust easily if the actor feels constricted and wants to do something differently. I tend to run long takes—playing out the scenes as far as I can reasonably take them.

I generally don't do a lot of close-ups because I like to see the environment around a person. I also don't shoot a lot of coverage. Harris and I had our shot list, but we'd remain open to what revealed itself on the day. Often we'd have other shots planned and not feel they were necessary.

You had a bigger budget this time. Did that change the way you work at all?

NB: The major difference was that I could change my mind on the day. *Squid* was a kind of kamikaze mission. We pretty much had to stick with the plan, and there was no going back if you didn't get what you wanted. I threw everything I had into that movie—it was a make-or-break thing. If I didn't get that right, I don't know if I would have had another shot. *Margot* was saner, but we maintained the energy that the shorter *Squid* shoot had, which I think is valuable. This is the model I would keep because it's enough money to do the movie properly, but not enough to get too comfortable.

CAST AND CREW CREDITS

PARAMOUNT VANTAGE Presents
A SCOTT RUDIN Production

A Film by
NOAH BAUMBACH

MARGOT AT THE WEDDING

NICOLE KIDMAN   JENNIFER JASON LEIGH   JACK BLACK   JOHN TURTURRO
CIARÁN HINDS   ZANE PAIS   FLORA CROSS   HALLEY FEIFFER

Written and Directed by NOAH BAUMBACH	Production Design by ANNE ROSS	Music Supervisor GEORGE DRAKOULIAS
Produced by SCOTT RUDIN	Edited by CAROL LITTLETON, ACE	Casting by DOUGLAS AIBEL
Director of Photography HARRIS SAVIDES, ASC	Costume Design by ANN ROTH	Co-Producer M. BLAIR BREARD

Cast
(In order of appearance)

Claude . . . . ZANE PAIS
Woman on Train . . SUSAN BLACKWELL
Margot . . . . NICOLE KIDMAN
Malcolm . . . . JACK BLACK
Ingrid . . . . FLORA CROSS
Pauline . . . . . JENNIFER JASON LEIGH
Toby . . . . SETH BARRISH
Alan . . . . MATTHEW ARKIN
Bruce . . . . BRIAN KELLEY
Fireman . . . . . . CHRISTIAN HANSEN
Mr. Vogler . . . . . . MICHAEL CULLEN
Mrs. Vogler . . . . ENID GRAHAM
Vogler Daughter . . . SOPHIE NYWEIDE
Vogler Son . . . . JUSTIN ROTH
Dick Koosman . . . . . . CIARÁN HINDS
Maisy Koosman . . . . . HALLEY FEIFFER
Malcolm's Friend . . . . JONATHAN
SCHWARTZ
Jim . . . . JOHN TURTURRO
Woman with Dog . . . . . . LISA EMERY
Karaoke Singer . . MICHAEL MEDEIROS
Becky . . . . ASHLIE ATKINSON

Crew

Unit Production Manager
. . . . M. BLAIR BREARD
First Assistant Director . . . . JOE CAMP III
First Assistant Director . . . JONO OLIVER
Second Assistant Director
. . . . MICHAEL T. MEADOR
Stunt Coordinator . . . . STEPHEN POPE
Stunts for Ms. Kidman
. . . . SHAWNNA THIBODEAU,
JODI MICHELLE PYNN
Production Supervisor . . DAVID BAUSCH
Art Director . . . ADAM STOCKHAUSEN
Graphic Design . . . . . PHILLIS LEHMER
Art Department Coordinator
. . . . PHILIP WINN
Set Decorator . . . . . DEBRA SCHUTT
Assistant Set Decorator . . . JENNY, ALEX,
NICK, ASON
Leadperson . . . . PHILIP CANFIELD
On-Set Dresser . . RUTH ANN DELEON
Set Dressers . . . . . . CHRIS FERRARO
CHRISTOPHER HEAPS
RICK HOPPE
Camera Operator . . . LUKASZ JOGALLA
First Assistant Camera
. . . . CHRISTOPHER BLAUVELT
Second Assistant Camera
. . . . DANIEL FEIGHERY
Film Loader
. . . . . CHRISTOPHER A. MOELLER
Still Photographer . . . . . KEN REGAN
Video Assist . . . . RICO ALSTON
Script Supervisor . . . . . MARY BAILEY
Sound Mixer . . . . DREW KUNIN

Boom Operator	KIRA SMITH
Sound Utility	JEANNE GILLILAND

Chief Lighting Technicians
.... JOHN VELEZ
BILL O'LEARY

Assistant Chief Lighting Technicians
.... DARRIN SMITH
JEREMY KNASTER

Electricians..... GARY HILDEBRAND
MICHAEL PAPADOPOULOS
MICHAEL P. PRISCO JR.
RYAN A. RODRIGUEZ
KABKEO PHOTHIVONGSA
PETER RUSSELL

First Company Grip . . KEVIN W. FLYNN
Second Company Grip
.... DAVID M. CARR
Dolly Grip ...... RONALD J. BURKE
Grips............ JOHN KRAUSE
WILLIAM MORAN
BOB A. VAN HEEK
TIMOTHY FLYNN
FRANZ YEICH

Costume Supervisor
.... DONNA M. MALONEY
Assistant Costume Designer
.... MICHELLE MATLAND
On-Set Costumer
.... NICOLE GREENBAUM
Ms. Kidman's Costumer.... IRIS LEMOS
Costume Assistant
.... JONATHAN SCHWARTZ
Costume Coordinator
.... EMILY GUNSHOR
Makeup Department Head
.... MICHAL BIGGER
Assistant Makeup Artist
.... PATRICIA REGAN
Makeup for Ms. Kidman
.... ANGELA LEVIN
Hair & Makeup for Mr. Black
.... ROZ MUSIC
Key Hair Designer.... LORI GUIDROZ
Hair Stylist to Ms. Kidman
.... WAYNE HERNDON
Hair Design for Ms. Kidman
.... KERRY WARN
Property Master... MARTIN LASOWITZ
Assistant Property Master
.... MICHAEL JORTNER
Property Assistant
.... ANA KATHARINA DRECHSLER
Special Effects Coordinator
.... STEVE KIRSHOFF

Special Effects Foreperson
.... FRANK OLIVA
Special Effects Technicians. . PHILIP BECK,
ANGEL TORRES, LORENZO T. HALL
Chief Greens........ WILL SCHECK
Greens..... GILBERT H. GERTSEN
GORDON H. GERTSEN
PETER LEVITSKY
Music Consultants... DEAN WAREHAM
BRITTA PHILLIPS
Title Design..... LEANNE SHAPTON
First Assistant Editor
.... MARTIN LEVENSTEIN
Post Production Supervisor
.... SARAH CONNORS
Post Production Assistant
.... JESSICA GREEN
Assistant Editor... ERNEST LEIF BOYD
Additional Assistant Editors
.... LYNN CASSANITI
BETH MORAN
Visual Effects by .... BIG FILM DESIGN
Visual Effects Supervisor
.... RANDY BALSMEYER
Visual Effects Artists
.... J. JOHN CORBETT
CHRIS HALSTEAD
Visual Effects Producer
.... TYRA HANSHAW
Sound Designer...... PAUL URMSON
First Assistant Sound Editor
.... RICK CHEFALAS
Dialogue Editor... JACK RUBENSTEIN
ADR Editors..... RUTH HERNANDEZ
GERALD DONLAN
Sound Effects Editor.. WYATT SPRAGUE
Apprentice Sound Editor
.... PALOMA MELE
Foley Editor...... STEVE VISSCHER
Foley Artist..... MARKO COSTANZO
Foley Mixer...... GEORGE A. LARA
Re-Recording Mixers... LEE DICHTER
PAUL URMSON
Additional Re-Recording Mixer
.... TOM FLEISCHMAN, CAS
Sound Re-Recordist.. LARRY HERMAN
ADR Mixer....... DOUG MURRAY
Post Production Sound Facility .. C5 INC.,
NEW YORK, NY
Mix Stage . . SOUND ONE, NEW YORK
Music Executive..... LINDA COHEN
Music Editor...... NANCY ALLEN
Assistants to Mr. Baumbach
..... JESSIE KILGUSS, CJ GARDELLA

Executive Assistant to Mr. Rudin
. . . . JAMES P. QUEEN
Assistants to Mr. Rudin
. . . . NATHAN KELLY,
ADAM MILCH, DANNY ROMAN
MARK ROTHMAN
Production Accountant . . SEAN HOGAN
First Assistant Accountant
. . . . FRANK MURRAY
Payroll Accountant . . SHELLIE GILLESPIE
Accounting Clerk . . . . . . AIDAN SHAH
Post Production Accountant
. . . . MICHELLE SARAMA
Location Manager . . . KEITH A. ADAMS
Assistant Location Manager
. . . . DAVID VELASCO
Scouts . . . . SUSAN SILAS
NILS WIDBOOM
Parking Coordinator
. . . . FRANCISCO MARCIAL
Production Coordinator. . . . ANITA SUM
Assistant Production Coordinator
. . . . PAMELA BERTINI
Production Secretaries
. . . . . CRAIG T. WOOD, ERIC DEAN
Second Second Assistant Directors
. . . . ANDREA O'CONNOR
KENYON NOBLE
Ms. Kidman's Dialect Coach
. . . . ELIZABETH
HIMELSTEIN-REYNOLDS
Assistants to Ms. Kidman
. . . . JUDY HEINZEN
GEMMA O'NEILL
Ms. Kidman's Security
. . . . WAYNE PETRUCELLI
Assistant to Ms. Leigh . . . . . SUSAN SOH
Assistant to Mr. Black
. . . . STEVE MORAMARCO
Office Production Assistants
. . . . HERNANDO BANSUELO
VINCENT PIOTTI
Film Runner . . . . . . NINA MAXWELL
Set Production Assistants . . KATE BOGLE
ALBERT MASSIAH
OAK PORCELLI
NORA RESNICK
KARA RYAN
MARK A. WILLS
Art Department Assistants
. . . . FRANCESCA MIRABELLA
LAURA NEMESI
Department Assistants . . . CHRIS CLOUD
SANTOS CORNIER

DEREK FRAMPTON DAVIS
KELLY MEYER DOUGLAS
ERICA FRANCIS
TRACY GOSSETT
SERENA KUO
LUIE MORALES
Casting Associate
. . . . STEPHANIE HOLBROOK
LA Casting Assistant
. . . . . DEBORAH MAXWELL DION
Background Casting . . . . . SYLVIA FAY/
LEE GENICK CASTING
Stand-Ins. . . . . KATE DALTON
KAT MURELLO
KATHY BERNARD
Medic . . . . LESLIE COLLINS
Unit Publicist . . . . ERIC MYERS
Dogs Provided by
. . . . DAWN ANIMAL AGENCY, INC.
Trainer . . . . BARBARA AUSTIN
Construction Coordinator
. . . . RICH HEBRANK
Chief Carpenter . . . PETER BUNDRICK
Chief Construction Grips
. . . . JONATHAN GRAHAM
RICHARD C. ROSE
Construction Grip . . . . PAT COCUZZO
Charge Scenics. . . . . ELIZABETH LINN
LISA MARIE KENNEDY
On-Set Painter . . . . . . BOB BARNETT
Scenic Foreperson . . . . . NILI LERNER
Shop Scenic . . . . ABE COSTANZA
Scenics . . . . STEPHEN BARTH
KATHLEEN B. DILKES
KRISTEN EMERY
NIR GAON, CAROLINE IRONS
LYNN NICKELS
STEVEN PURTEE
MARIAN ZIOLA-STOEFFELMEIER
Transportation Captain . . GENE O'NEILL
Transportation Co-Captain
. . . . JOHN CANAVAN
Drivers. . . . . . . ERNIE ACQUEVILLA,
THOMAS AQUINO, WILLIAM BAKER,
PATRICK J. BENTZ,
EDWARD J. BUZZO,
MIKE CANALE, DAVID CHACON,
JAMES CHARLESTON, CHARLES FAY,
JOSEPH FAY, KEVIN GRIFFIN,
DIMITRI JACOTIN, ADRIAN KEENAN,
JOHN LALOR, JESSE LELLO,
MARK EDWARD MAY,
JOSEPH PAPROTA, WES PETERSEN
Catering by . . TRIBE ROAD CATERING

Craft Service . . THOMSON BROTHERS
Clearance by. . . . CLEARANCE DOMAIN
Dailies Telecine
. . . CREATIVE MEGA PLAYGROUND
Dailies Advisor . . . . . JOEY VIOLANTE
Dailies by
. . . . . TECHNICOLOR NEW YORK
Color Timer. . . . . . STEVE SHERIDAN
Negative Cutter
. . . . MARY NELSON-FRASER
Dolby Sound Consultant . . PAUL SACCO
Titles and Opticals by
. . . PACIFIC TITLE AND ART STUDIO

"NORTHERN BLUE"
Written & Performed by Dean Wareham
& Britta Phillips

"ROMEO'S TUNE"
Written & Performed by Steve Forbert
Courtesy of Nemperor Records

"GO TELL AUNT RHODY"
Traditional Performed by Jack Black

"GENESIS"
Written & Performed by Jorma Kaukonen
Courtesy of Columbia Records
By arrangement with Sony BMG
Music Entertainment

"ONE FINE SUMMER MORNING"
Written by Al Gorgoni
Performed by Evie Sands
Courtesy of A&M Records
Under license from Universal Music Enterprises

"GOIN' DOWN TO LAUREL"
Written & Performed by Steve Forbert
Courtesy of Nemperor Records

"THE WAGON"
Written by Joseph Mascis
Performed by Dinosaur Jr.
Courtesy of Warner Music UK
By arrangement with Warner Music Group
Film & TV Licensing

"DEAR MARY"
Written by Steven H. Miller
Performed by Steve Miller Band
Courtesy of Capitol Records
Under license from EMI Film
& Television Music

"SEE HOW WE ARE"
Written by Exene Cervenka and John Doe
Performed by X
Courtesy of Elektra Entertainment Group
By arrangement with Warner Music Group
Film & TV Licensing

"SUNDAY GIRL"
Written by Christopher Stein
Performed by Zane Pais

"EVERYTHING CHANGES"
Written & Performed by Lesley Duncan
Courtesy of Lesley Duncan

"UNION CITY BLUE"
Written by Deborah Harry and
Nigel Harrison
Performed by Blondie
Courtesy of Capitol Records
Under license from EMI Film
& Television Music

"YOU AND ME"
Written by Alice Cooper and Dick Wagner
Performed by Alice Cooper
Courtesy of Warner Bros. Records Inc.
By arrangement with Warner Music Group
Film & TV Licensing

"CLAIR"
Written & Performed by Gilbert O'Sullivan
Courtesy of Grand Upright Music Ltd.

"EASY TO BE AROUND"
Written & Performed by Diane Cluck
Courtesy of Diane Cluck

"NOTHING IS WRONG"
Written by Peter Holsapple
Performed by The dB's
Courtesy of Capitol Records
Under license from EMI Film
& Television Music
And Courtesy of Line Music GmbH

"THAT'S ALL FOR EVERYONE"
Written by Lindsey Buckingham
Performed by Fleetwood Mac
Courtesy of Warner Bros. Records Inc.
By arrangement with
Warner Music Group
Film & TV Licensing

"ON AND ON"
Written by Stephen Bishop
Performed by Michael Medeiros

"TEEN ANGEL"
Written by Donovan Leitch
Performed by Donovan
Courtesy of Epic Records
By arrangement with Sony BMG
Music Entertainment
And Licensed Courtesy of EMI Records Ltd.

"SOMETHING ON YOUR MIND"
Written by Dino Valenti
Performed by Karen Dalton
Courtesy of HLLMS, LLC & Light In
The Attic Records

The Producers wish to thank the following:
THE CITY OF NEW YORK
MAYOR'S OFFICE OF FILM, THEATRE,
AND BROADCASTING
VILLAGE OF SOUTHAMPTON
HAMPTON BAYS FIRE DEPARTMENT
ME & RO JEWELRY
STIHL
TYLER GRAPHICS

Special thanks to:
BARBARA TURNER

This is a carbon neutral production:
100% of carbon emissions offset with
Native Energy

AMERICAN HUMANE ASSOCIATION
monitored the animal action.
(AHA 01246)

KODAK
Motion Picture Film

Color by deluxe®
Deluxe Laboratories

Filmed with Arri® Cameras
Lenses provided by DuClos Lenses

DOLBY DIGITAL®
In Selected Theatres
DTS™

SDDS™
Sony Dynamic Digital Sound
In Selected Theatres

Financing in part provided by
MARATHON FUNDING LLC

Copyright © MMVII by PARAMOUNT
VANTAGE,
A Division of PARAMOUNT PICTURES
All Rights Reserved.

THE PERSONS AND EVENTS IN THIS MOTION
PICTURE ARE FICTITIOUS. ANY SIMILARITY TO
ACTUAL PERSONS OR EVENTS IS UNINTENTIONAL.

THIS MOTION PICTURE IS PROTECTED UNDER
LAWS OF THE UNITED STATES AND OTHER
COUNTRIES. UNAUTHORIZED DUPLICATION,
DISTRIBUTION OR EXHIBITION MAY RESULT IN
CIVIL LIABILITY AND CRIMINAL PROSECUTION.

MPAA # 43243   IATSE
MOTION PICTURE ASSOCIATION
OF AMERICA

ABOUT THE WRITER/DIRECTOR

NOAH BAUMBACH wrote and directed *The Squid and the Whale* in 2005 and received an Oscar® nomination for Best Original Screenplay. He won screenplay awards from the New York Film Critics Circle, the National Society of Film Critics, the Los Angeles Film Critics Association, the National Board of Review, and the Toronto Film Critics Association. *The Squid and the Whale* also won Best Picture from the New York Critics Online and received three Golden Globe nominations, including Best Picture, as well as six Independent Spirit Award nominations, including Best Picture. Baumbach also wrote and directed *Kicking and Screaming,* and co-wrote *The Life Aquatic with Steve Zissou*. He has written for *The New Yorker* magazine.